Jan Kerouac:
A Life in Memory

Jan Kerouac:
A Life in Memory

EDITED BY GERALD NICOSIA

For Bruce Hodder —
A TRue Beat,
who carries The flame
forward in
love + truth —
your friend,
Gerry Nicosia
4-17-09
Corte
Madera,
California

NOODLEBRAIN PRESS

Library of Congress Cataloging-in-Publication Data

Nicosia, Gerald, 1949—

    Jan Kerouac: a life in memory / Gerald Nicosia

    ISBN 978-0-615-24554-6 (paperback)

  1. Kerouac, Jan, 1952-1996. 2. Kerouac, Jack, 1922-1969. 3. Authors, American—20th century—Biography. 4. Beat Generation—Biography. I. Title.

Library of Congress catalog number applied for

First Edition

Published by Noodlebrain Press

PO Box 130

Corte Madera, CA 94976-0130

Cover photo: Jan Kerouac in Hollywood, 1978. Photographer unknown.

Frontispiece photo: Jan Kerouac working on *Baby Driver*, Hollywood, 1978. Photo by Marie-Andrée Cossette.

Cameo photo: Jan Kerouac in Hollywood, 1978. Photo by Marie-Andrée Cossette.

This book is dedicated to the memory of
Stanley Twardowicz, whom Jack Kerouac called
"the most compassionate man I ever met"

CONTENTS

ACKNOWLEDGMENTS

There are so many people to thank for helping make this book happen. First and foremost, thanks to the Kerouac Family Association, known in French as L'Association des Familles Kirouac. Two members of that association, in particular, have been critical in keeping my work on Jan Kerouac alive and flourishing: Jacques Kirouac, the founding president, and J. A. Michel Bornais, the current secretary. Kudos to designer Luz Decker and to all who contributed, in various ways, to see that Jan Kerouac's life story was preserved in print. Of course, great thanks to all who contributed their photos and memoirs of Jan Kerouac. Special thanks to Phil Cousineau, who worked diligently to edit Jan's not-quite-complete draft of *Parrot Fever* into publishable form. *Gracias a* Alejandro Murguia for Spanish translations. Thanks to Sisyphus Press, *Le Trésor des Kirouac,* the *Chicago Sun-Times*, and all other publications where pieces of this book may have previously been published. Thanks to James Barrios and DeHart's Media Services for a sympathetic understanding of this project all the way through. Thanks to all who have loved Jan Kerouac, those who still love her, and those around the world who cherish her work—for refusing to let her be forgotten. And thanks most of all to the lady herself, and lady she was, as well as writer extraordinaire, and noodlebrain too ("I say that reveringly," to quote her): Janet Michelle Kerouac.

—G. N., July 16, 2008, Corte Madera, California

INTRODUCTION

by Gerald Nicosia

Twelve years ago, I got the phone call from Albuquerque telling me that Jan Kerouac was dead. I didn't even know she was in the hospital, or I would have flown down to be at her side. I had talked to her less than a week before. I knew she had grown weak, from problems with her spleen and platelet count that derived ultimately from the kidney failure she had suffered in January of 1991. She had just recently moved from her own rented house to a nursing home, but she was hoping to regain her strength in time for the scheduled trial of the lawsuit she had filed against the Sampas family, alleging that they had forged her grandmother's will. It was Gabrielle Kerouac's will—leaving everything to Stella Sampas Kerouac, Jack Kerouac's third wife—that had kept Jan from inheriting any of her father's literary estate. The trial was set for September, 1996. But on June 5, 1996, her "ex-sister-in-law" (as Jan liked to call her) Deborah Lash Bower chose to remove Jan from life support less than 24 hours after the surgery she'd just had to remove her spleen. No longer bound for the trial in St. Petersburg, Florida, that she had counted upon to vindicate all her struggles of the past two years, Jan Kerouac, at the too-young age of 44, was now among the angels. There were more than a few of us, though, who had suspected she was an angel all along.

I suppose there are those who will ask why a book about her should be published now. Even one so august as Carolyn Cassady, who at one time praised Jan's literary talent, told me she felt this book was

11

superfluous because "Jan had *nothing whatever* to do with her father's life."

It is true Jan met Jack Kerouac only twice—and spoke to him one additional time in a long, drunken (on his end) telephone call. But he—or perhaps more accurately, his absence—dominated her whole life. During those last, lonely years of endless legal and medical battles, she always kept a shrine to Jack (and sometimes to both her parents) in whatever rented home she lived in. The shrine contained his books, his pictures, a candle, and a few other things that reflected his memory. She would have added the cork from his bottle of Harvey's Bristol Cream sherry, she told me, but she had lost it long ago.

She was always at pains to tell people that she did not blame Jack for abandoning and denying her—that she understood he was "doing something more important" than being a father. But a few months before she died, she exploded in an uncharacteristic rage and smashed the altar to her father—she told me over the phone—because she felt that most of the pain and grief in her life were his fault. As was typical of her, she did not hold on to that anger long. Within a few days she was again speaking—and telling interviewers like Todd Bauer, who came down from Chicago to videotape her—that she wanted to be remembered as "the daughter who saved her father's archive."

But this book comes from more than the fact that Jan Kerouac was a key part of Jack Kerouac's life—even if only "the missing element," as she liked to say, who "enabled him to be who he was." She was indisputably a tremendous writer in her own right, and her work needs to be revived, read, and studied as the contribution of a major post-Beat writer herself. She was a born writer, who loved storytelling and loved, above all, words and the endless semantic and symbolic games she could play with them. I remember how when the two of us stayed by ourselves for a couple of weeks (in September 1978) in the house of Stanley and Lil Twardowicz on Long Island, Jan would sometimes open a dictionary in the evening and begin creating games with it—challenging me to define new words and daring me to try to find words she couldn't define. It was one of her favorite forms of entertainment, along with surfing encyclopedia entries (long before there was an internet) to find people, places, and things she'd never heard of.

Mainly, though, this book comes as a response to the fact that Jan Kerouac—both her life and her work, indeed her very existence—

is being systematically erased from literary history. That may sound like a strong statement, but the truth of it is even more dreadful than it sounds. That attempt to expunge her began even when she was alive—when, for instance, she was not allowed to speak at New York University's conference on her father in 1995. She was, in fact, made to pay $120 just to get in the door, and then was forcibly removed by police when she "dared" to ask Allen Ginsberg for permission to address the audience for a few minutes about the need to preserve her father's literary archive intact in a library. There sat Kerouac Estate executor John Sampas, right next to NYU's Program Director Helen Kelly, yelling viciously, and perhaps even gleefully, "Get her out of here!"

There is enough evidence of the blacklisting of Jan Kerouac by the Kerouac Estate to fill a book. Let me just mention a few salient examples here. In her last years, Jan had struggled with all her failing powers to finish her third novel, *Parrot Fever*, the final installment of her autobiographical trilogy that began with *Baby Driver* (1981) and then expanded thematically with *Trainsong* (1988). She had almost completed *Parrot Fever* at the time of her death. During my three-year tenure as her literary executor (a job I was forced from after the combined team of John Sampas and Jan's heirs, ex-husband John Lash and half-brother David Bowers, spent something like $400,000 in legal fees to oust me and, hence, prevent me from carrying Jan's legal case to trial), I forged an agreement with Thunder's Mouth Press to publish the book. Some of the memoirs in this present book were actually commissioned to be published along with the slender text of *Parrot Fever*. The book's publication was eventually cancelled, at least in part, due to John Lash's pressuring Thunder's Mouth Press not to publish it. That is what I was told, at any rate, by the press's former publisher Neil Ortenberg. (For the record, John Lash had allied himself with John Sampas and the Kerouac Estate within weeks after Jan died—a fact that came out in the probate battle over Jan's estate in Albuquerque.)

A year ago, Jack Kerouac's hometown of Lowell, Massachusetts, held a celebration centering on his roll manuscript of *On the Road*. (Jack Kerouac did not call it a "scroll," a term the Sampas family invented.) As part of this exhibit, overseen by John Sampas, there was a so-called "Kerouac Family Wall" of photos. There was not a single photo of Jan on that family wall.

Only a few months ago, the New York Public Library held one

13

of the largest and longest exhibitions on Jack Kerouac's life and work ever staged—once more centering on the roll manuscript of *On the Road*. And again, from what I was told by people who attended it, there was not a single mention in the exhibition of Jan Kerouac, the writer's only child, both begotten and born legitimately during his marriage to his second wife Joan Haverty—a child who was "in the womb," as she liked to say, while her dad was still tinkering with that first draft of his seminal Beat novel.

I know of what I speak in regard to blacklists, as I have been subjected to one myself ever since I supported Jan Kerouac's lawsuit against the Sampas family. For those who doubt my claims on this, I suggest they try to find any mention of me or my groundbreaking Kerouac biography *Memory Babe* anywhere in Howard Cunnell's recent, copiously annotated "scroll edition" of *On the Road*, a book whose publication originated with—and would not have been possible without the permission of—John Sampas. *Memory Babe* is not even listed in Cunnell's bibliography, which contains the titles of numerous other works on Kerouac, many of which include citations to *Memory Babe* in their own bibliographies.

I might also suggest the doubters turn to page 566 of Bill Morgan's recent biography of Allen Ginsberg, *I Celebrate Myself*. In a paragraph where now sits a brief, cryptic reference to a "new Kerouac biography," there had been in Morgan's manuscript a long passage quoting Ginsberg's reactions in his journal upon first reading *Memory Babe*—a highly laudatory paragraph that had concluded with Ginsberg's assessment of *Memory Babe* as a "great book."

Both of those books, Cunnell's and Morgan's, were—not coincidentally—published by Viking Penguin, the Sampas family's publisher of choice, and for whom the Sampas family's Kerouac copyrights make oodles and oodles of money.

Let none of this be construed as indicating a raison d'être for this book in vindictiveness. Nor is the book in your hands an attempt to further Jan Kerouac's lawsuit against the Sampas family for the forgery of her grandmother's will, though the lawsuit still limps along, carried on as best as possible by Jan's cousin, Jack Kerouac's nephew, Paul Blake, Jr., who has been both destitute and homeless for large portions of his life. At this point, the Sampases have spent a small fortune in legal fees to keep that case from ever going to trial. And no wonder. The evidence I have seen—including handwriting analysis, the recanting of a witness, and medical testimony about Gabrielle's inability to sign a will—all seem compellingly on Jan's side.

That the case is still alive at all is due to the persistence, courage, and integrity of Paul Blake, Jr.'s lawyer, Bill Wagner of Wagner, Vaughan, and McLaughlin in Orlando, Florida—who has worked diligently for more than eleven years against a phalanx of well-paid Sampas family attorneys for a client who cannot pay him dollar one.

But again, all this more properly belongs to another story—a saga with its own cast of heroes and villains—which God willing will be told someday.

No, if I wage any kind of war here, it is to preserve the memory of this incredibly intelligent, gifted, generous, and good-hearted young woman, Jan Kerouac—"more sinned against than sinning"—against the disregard that is being deliberately and unfairly foisted on her. As long as I live, I will not let the world forget that she existed, or that she stood for the truths and good things—justice for the poor and downtrodden, above all—that she did. That is a promise I made to Jan herself while she was alive.

There are omissions in this book, especially from the scenes of her early life, though Jan wrote about much of it in *Baby Driver* and also covered a lot of the events in the long interview I did with her for the *Chicago Sun-Times* in 1979, which is printed at the very end. No attempt is made here at a complete biography—though one can't help hoping such a book will eventually be written. It seemed more important at the present moment to get out some kind of memoir of her— even an incomplete and mosaic one—before the continuing snowfall of oblivion (to steal a metaphor from her beloved Joyce) buried her beyond recovery.

I hope that what you read of her here will give you some sense of the real person who lived behind and underneath the incredibly heavy burden of the name Janet Michelle Kerouac. Even on her gravestone they got her name wrong. There she is labeled and misspelled "Jan Michele." Moreover, I hope that what you read herein will make you like this young woman, at least a little, or intrigue you enough that you will be driven to read what she wrote—for that is the legacy she cared most to leave us.

—G. N., Mill Valley, California, July 1, 2008

EDITOR'S NOTE

I knew Jan Kerouac for almost twenty years, and I have thousands of memories of her. When I first met her, she was 26 years old, a black-haired, blue-eyed, scintillating beauty. She was bright, very articulate, and very funny. She loved to camp, to mug, to make faces, to joke, to put people on with extravagant fake stories. She was absolute fun to be around. But I also found that she had a very dark and unhappy side. One day, having lunch in a New York City restaurant, I asked her what her destiny would be. I was wondering if she thought she would become a famous writer, as she was then completing her first novel, *Everthreads* (later published as *Baby Driver*).

Jan said, "My destiny is to be pulverized." I almost fell out of my chair. She was not joking that time. She was dead serious. She did not believe she would live long, and she felt she would be forgotten, dying unloved and unknown. She did die young, but she was wrong about the other two things. When she died, she was loved by many people who knew the pure-hearted little girl inside the wild young woman; and she was not unknown. She had written three excellent novels—the last one, *Parrot Fever*, still unfortunately not published—and she would be remembered, as she wished, as "the daughter who tried to save her father's archive" from the people who were selling it off piecemeal to collectors and dealers around the world. She wanted her father's papers preserved in a library, not sold off to the highest bidder for hard cash. That battle still goes on.

I remember her poetry, her stories, her exuberant love of life and how much she loved language, loved learning new words and new languages, loved exploring new places she had never been. I also remember her passion for justice, for the poor and outsiders. She was always railing against the American Congress and the Republican Party for cutting off monetary subsidies and welfare for the poor. She also loved all animals and was outraged at the destruction of our earthly environment. Most of all, she cared about everyone she met. She did not play the "famous daughter," but was accessible to all, talked to everyone who came up to her, answered every letter that anyone sent her. She felt she had received a great gift in being Jack Kerouac's daughter, and she wanted to share this with the world. And, in fact, she has done so, and is still doing that through her writings and all the efforts she made to preserve the Kerouac Archive.

As her literary executor, by her instructions, I placed all of her own papers at the Bancroft Library, University of California, Berkeley, where they can be studied by all future generations.

—Gerald Nicosia

Phil Cousineau

THE NIGHT I DROVE KEROUAC HOME

"Anyway, the time has come to explain the Golden Eternity ..."
— Jack Kerouac

The amber lights flicker past as we slip across the long stretch of the Golden Gate Bridge. The twin towers loom above us like colossal sentinels. Foghorns moan across the bay.

Jan stares mournfully at the *neon redly twinkling* of the *white city of San Francisco on her eleven mystic hills*, as her father described it on the long roll of drawing paper that became the notorious runaway novel.

I tell her how much I was moved by her story at Gerry Nicosia's dinner party about the first time she read her father's work. Through the haze of her fourth dialysis treatment of the day she had described how she was twelve years old and in the hospital for a drinking problem. Her doctor noticed the name "Kerouac" on her medical chart. On a hunch, he asked if she was related to the famous writer. She shrugged. He asked if she'd read any of his books. Petulantly, she shook her head no. A few minutes later, he returned with a copy of *On the Road*, which he handed to her and said, "Read it. It might help."

She told us all this with a tang of regret. "I was up all night," she'd said with end-of-the-world weariness. "By the time I finished I finally understood why my father was never around while I was growing up."

As we pass under the mighty towers of the bridge, I confess to her that I didn't get around to reading it until I was twenty-two. I was languishing in London, working for a professor of literature who thought I needed a jolt to get me, well, on the road again. He climbed the Victorian library ladder in his reading room and pulled down a leather-bound edition of *Seven Pillars of Wisdom* by T. E. Lawrence, a history of the English Secret Service, and a first edition of Kerouac's *On the Road*.

"Your Dad's book was a kind of hurricane for me," I reveal to her. I plunge ahead into No Man's Land, trying to convey the way I felt when all those wind-blown words and bebopping rhythms helped catapult me around the world. Emboldened, I tell her how his *holy goof zany lunacy words* helped vault me into the world of writing.

A wry smile crosses her face. "Everyone remembers the first time they read that one," she says with sudden childlike exuberance. Her eyes flash with momentary delight, then she asks, "But where are they now?" Implying, when his daughter could use some help.

Jan's fingers drum nervously on the window molding of the car door. She seems ravaged by the mean mix of health and literary problems, the struggle to finish her third novel, *Parrot Fever*, and the bitter fight over her father's literary estate. She looks like she's only longing for the quiet anonymity of her motel room.

Slowly, her attention drifts away. She gazes out at the silver wake left by a ship far out at sea. Her sad face is cast in an eerie silhouette that slowly shape-shifts into the spitting image of her father.

For one phantasmagorical moment he's leaning back in the passenger seat of my knockabout '82 Mustang, all peripatetic, poetic, and beat, to paraphrase the playwright. It's Jack ever-lovin' Kerouac, slick and slack in his brown leather jacket, the original coolhunter, wistful in his world of hurt, caught in some dharma bum time-warp between love affairs, tumbledown motels, ramshackle bars, and the long loping backroads, as he wrote, of *bluer than eternity Wildamerica*.

In this one crazy Roman candle instant he's staring across the dark bay, longing for the loony locomotion of the open road, digging the long blues line of the distant lowing foghorn on Alcatraz, marveling at the glorious memories of driving his holy goof buddy, Neal Cassady, in an old juddering jalopy under a night-gliding moon, past *groves of lonesome redwood trees*, over boundless plains and beyond the great lakes, listening for bone-deep cries of jazzmen who just might *raise men's souls to joy.* All the while they're reading from the bluesy manuscript of night like a couple of Zen drunk monks, maddashing into the heart of strange roads at the crackling of the blue dawn.

Go moan, go moan for man, go moan, I hear in the jeweled weirdness.

And now Jan's smoky voice lures me back from my reverie. "So I guess my father wasn't around because he was roaring back and forth across the country, driving like a madman, then sitting in a dark room for months writing about it. He didn't seem to have time for anything or anybody else. Even me. When I figured that out I was finally able to forgive him."

I ask if she has any other memories of him. With disarming shyness she says, "I remember him coming into my room when I was a little girl and whispering *'Shush!'* to my little sisters so he wouldn't wake me. But that's all I remember except for one other short visit when I was in my teens.

"It's not much," she concludes with a dash of her father's *doomtragic* inflection. "But I'll take whatever I can get."

I downshift for the tollbooth and root around in my vest pocket for some change.

"I'm so tired," Kerouac's daughter says with her father's *end of the continent sadness.* Her voice is stretched on the rack of night. "I'm so tired of being sick. I don't expect to be around forever, you know."

Her voice catches in her throat, as it did earlier in the night, at Nicosia's, when she told us what happened when she made the pilgrimage to her father's last home, in Florida, in 1994. At first she was frail and vulnerable in the telling, but she gained strength as she revealed how she felt "at home." After serving tea, the new owner, John Sampas, brother of Jack's last wife, asked if he could get her anything else. In her inimitable way she said exactly what was on her mind. She said she'd love to have her father's rolltop desk. The response was mocking. "That's the way the cookie crumbles, Jan." She was crushed. She owned nothing of her father's. Listening, it seemed to me that she'd come to live by her father's *go moan for man* words as if they were a mad prophecy.

We pass like phantoms through the toll booth and drive on through the marbleized mist shrouding the Presidio, past the darkly floating boats of the Marina. Once again, Jack's words float back to

me, summoned by the force of his daughter's inconsolable loneliness—
happiness consists in realizing that it all is a great strange dream—and
by the city that inspired *a thousand dreams of zest.*

When we suddenly reach the bright and garish lights of the Holiday Inn on the Wharf, I drop her off, promising to look her up someday
in Albuquerque. Jan nods, grievously, then vanishes into the *motel, motel, motel loneliness* her father knew all too well, one more cursed child
of the famous and legendary. As she hesitantly closes the door behind
her, I imagine *locomotives wailing all night long.*

I want to say something to her through the window: Go on, press
on, regardless, everything depends on those who go on. But I let her go,
silently, remembering her old man's nearly last words:

But, no matter, anyway, the road is life . . . .

San Francisco, California, June 1995 (first published in *The Book of
Roads* by Phil Cousineau, Sisyphus Press, 2000)

Adiel Gorel

TRAVELS WITH JAN:
THE GIRL WITH THAT SPECIAL *PING*!

I first met Jan Kerouac in Mexico. It was about 1985. We were both traveling. I actually met her boyfriend first. He introduced me to her.

The three of us had a blast. I quickly realized how funny she was. We spent most of our time roaring with laughter about everything. She adored Spanish, even though she hadn't really mastered it. She loved puns, and if the pun could be bilingual—all the better.

Jan was the kind of person with whom my own humor just kept bubbling near the surface. Some people have that effect on you. She was not only a great listener but a great observer. She retained an enormous amount. I later saw our first encounter described in her book *Trainsong*. Heck, she used an entire paragraph just to describe my accent!

After the first Mexican encounter Jan and I kept in touch. We met again in Mexico and traveled together for awhile. Again her intelligent, attentive presence was such an enabler for others' intelligence, as her humor was an enabler for others' wit. She could refer to the most mundane bit of life and include it in a larger, creative context. One almost trivial example is, she liked the way the Mexicana Airlines crew made the usual mandatory announcements before a flight takes off. At the end of the announcements there is a little *ping!* sound—perhaps from the mike being turned off. Jan loved to play with that announcement, and she most certainly never missed the *ping!* She would weave it into other contexts, always with great hilarity. There were hundreds of other such examples.

I liked the fact that Jan could span such a wide spectrum: she was completely down to earth and could bum it with the best of them, traveling with very little money and staying at the most basic places. She could also feel comfortable at special readings in her honor or her father's honor. I remember a big event at City Lights bookstore in San Francisco. She was just as at home there, being the center of attention, as she was hitchhiking on a dirt road. There was once a major event in her honor in San Francisco—a series of benefit concerts and performances. I think it was three days long. Jan was as easily gracious getting the honors and accolades as anywhere else. She always had this "half asleep" quality to her, but she was extremely alert and picked up everything.

She couldn't escape her last name. Everywhere people got a kick when they realized she was Jack Kerouac's daughter. Being a writer herself probably made it even harder to step outside his oversized shadow. At times I would meet her with some friends, and I could see they were awed by being around Kerouac's daughter. I am sure she would have preferred for them to be awed just by being with her.

Jan visited me in Palo Alto, where I used to live, and then in Marin County, where I moved. Towards her later years she had a hard time, as her kidneys were failing her. One night I came to pick her up from a friend's house in San Anselmo. I was with my sister and brother-in-law who were visiting, and we were all going to go to The Stinking Rose restaurant in San Francisco. My sister and her husband waited outside while I went in to get Jan. She was cursing heavily and was clearly frustrated. She was almost having a dialogue with her illness, saying things along the lines of, "You are not gonna keep me at home! I WILL go out and have fun! I am gonna do what I want!" It saddened me.

Jan used to send me funny postcards from places she'd be, usually with art by her and some funny lines (maybe even the ever-present "ping"). She was a good friend. Even if I wouldn't see her for a long time, it still felt as if we had just seen each other. I know it's a corny thing to say, but this is how it really felt. She kept in touch. I wasn't so good at keeping in touch, but she was good enough for both of us.

Jan told me at various times about battles she was having regarding her father's estate. Not knowing too many details, my feelings were that Jan didn't stand a chance. She was the last person I saw dealing with legal issues, legal battles, and the like. Jan had a lot of the old 60's and 70's "free spirit." I thought that no matter what the details of the battle would be, she would most likely be short-changed.

During the time I knew her, Jan was working on a new book called *Parrot Fever*. I was very curious to read it. First, I knew that the ever-observant, brilliant Jan would create a gripping tale. I also knew that some of our mutual adventures were likely to appear in the book and was dying to read how she presented them. I was very disappointed when I heard that her book would not be published. Once again, I guess Jan lost the battle. Even post-mortem. I hope someone will pick up her manuscript and publish it.

I hope my words serve as a small ode to a good friend, a fascinating person, of pure and child-like spirit, and a brilliant mind. I miss you Jan, and you will never be forgotten.

John Zielinski

THE BABE WHO BROKE MY HEART

It was the late '70's. I was a medical student at Northwestern University, and I had two personalities. By day, I dissected cadavers and memorized endless chains of biochemical reactions until I was blue in the face, but by 10 PM you could find me at the Jazz Showcase on Chicago's famed Rush Street or at one of the many bars on Lincoln Avenue.

In those days Lincoln Park was a real mix, and my apartment was only a few blocks away. I had a lot of friends in the bars: poets, junkies, old guys who smoked pipes and the occasional former SDS-er, tripped out on LSD. One night at Katz's [the Katzenjammer Bar] my friend Gerry Nicosia walked in with Skip, a cartoon artist who worked for *Playboy* magazine, and a beautiful brunette. Gerry had written Jack Kerouac's biography, *Memory Babe*, best of many according to the *London Times*, and the babe with him was Jack's daughter, Jan.

We all sat at a table, and within a few minutes I was in love. Besides her sparkling smile and blue eyes, she had high blood pressure and assorted medical problems. I was going to be her doctor, maybe more, I thought to myself. It started to snow. Did she need a ride someplace, I asked? We all jumped into my big yellow '71 Mercury and spun out into slippery traffic. I stopped to get a pack of cigarettes; and when I got back, she was in the cavernous back seat, necking with Skip and smoking a joint.

I guess a lot of dreams end that way. Gerry and I have been friends ever since.

[EDITOR'S NOTE: I think my friend Dr. John, as we call him, may have conflated two separate visits. Jan first stopped to see me in Chicago on a cross-country bus trip in November, 1978, when she was leaving Stone Ridge, New York, after a brief visit to her old friend Carol Shank, and was on her way to live with her mother in Ellensburg, Washington. It did snow during that visit. Then Jan came back to Chicago for a longer stay with me in June of 1979, when I introduced her at the national convention of the National Society of Arts and Letters at the posh Ritz-Carlton Hotel. My memory is that we went to *Playboy* and met Skip during the June visit. Skip certainly came on to her, and she later told me that he wanted to sleep with her, with the implication—or so she felt—that he could do something for her at *Playboy*. But Judith Wax of *Playboy* had already rejected the chapter of *Everthreads* which I had sent her, saying she had no use for an "*On the Road* with Jack's daughter." And Jan told me that she was long past the era of sleeping with men to get favors, for her career or otherwise.

My main memory of that night at the Katz was that Jan decided to demonstrate to us how she used to hustle pool in New Mexico. She had on a black-and-white polka-dot minidress, and her black hair was permed (for the Ritz-Carlton banquet) and down past her shoulders. The unsuspecting guy she challenged to a game of pool was far too smitten by her looks to think much about the twenty-dollar bet she made with him; then she dispatched her balls in short order, and the guy paid up, but was clearly pissed off to have been beaten so badly by a 100-pound babe in a polka-dot minidress. Since she was with the three of us (and Skip was big and burly enough to make up for the diminutive stature of Dr. John and myself), the guy didn't make too much of a fuss. But Jan later confided to us that in New Mexico the macho Hispanic guys would sometimes flip out when she'd beat them at pool, and she said one time she literally had to fight off an angry pool player with her pool cue, in a kind of swashbuckling sword fight a la Douglas Fairbanks. It ended, if I remember right, with both of them crashing through a plate-glass window.]

Lee Harris

JANNY KERRACKY AND THE TURQUOISE POOLS

The all-American girl shot heroin at thirteen. The snap of bubble gum and steady stream of Shirelles and Lesley Gore records had given way to stealing money and food, and the dope took some of the sting out of Lower East Side slum life. She even resorted, sometimes, to teenage prostitution, a la Jodie Foster in *Taxi Driver*. Only for less dinero and no DeNiro.

And it all took place about seven miles south of where her father and his pals had launched a literary revolution—Kerouac, Ginsberg, Burroughs, thumbing their noses at the grayhairs of Columbia University, an age ago. In their suits, top coats, and fedora hats, they don't look much like revolutionaries in the photos that survive. For barefoot street urchin Janet Michelle Kerouac in 1965, they surely would have seemed like coddled academicians, and 1947 would definitely have been an age ago.

I'd like to pull some clever reversal on *On the Road* and say, "I first met Jan not long after my first wife and I split up," but in reality I first met her not long after my second wife and I married. Her medical and legal expenses were mounting, and Gerry Nicosia had asked me if I could come up to San Francisco in June 1995 for a series of Jan benefits. I would be his Man Friday, running errands, picking up people at the airport, and driving Jan to interviews and back to her hotel for her kidney dialysis.

My first meeting with her was over the phone, she at her hotel and I at Gerry's house. My voice actor's ear identified her right away as Jack Kerouac's daughter, detecting what I later called her inherited "big lippies," tasting every syllable with the same easygoing deliberation associated with her Dad. When I pointed this out, she knew immediately what I meant and started elongating her vowels so that she *really* sounded like Jack!

Rambling around San Francisco over the next several days, Jan and I talked little of her father and became fast friends. Our flippant natures provided an emollient barrier to the vast seriousness of everything—as in Ginsberg's "America," boy were things serious. Her health, her legal problems, the interviews and readings, and being accosted, as she had been her whole life, about the father she'd met twice.

I thought about 1955. Jan was three, and there would be no *On the Road* published, and no me, for another two years. Kerouac's favorite bar, "the one and only *Third and Howard*!" had been bulldozed in the seventies urban renewal south of Market Street. My air-conditioned Mercury Topaz paled in coolness compared to Detroit's postwar chrome mountains; I was no Neal Cassady, and I was with a girl Kerouac. And while Kenneth Rexroth had presided over the ferment of the San Francisco Poetry Renaissance in the Eisenhower era, poor Gerry was losing his mind dealing with the details and disparate hippie buffoons in this effort to help Jan.

The benefits were successful, concluding with the big Saturday night at Fort Mason. I left just before the show started, and in the parking lot Jan introduced me briefly to her cousin Paul (Jack's sister Nin's son). I crossed the Bay Bridge and peeled out on the 400 miles to Los Angeles, and Jan returned to her home in Albuquerque a while later.

Throughout the summer and fall of 1995, we had many lengthy phone conversations about how our family backgrounds had screwed us up, and about The Jack Kerouac Corporation of America. For that's what it had become, an impenetrable monolith whose only purpose was to make money (and not for Jan). Worse, it had gained the complicity of Ginsberg, not only in sanitizing and embalming Jack's legacy as part of the New York literary establishment, but in shutting Jan out of the process completely. (It was Ginsberg who led the effort to have Jan physically removed by the police from the 1995 NYU conference on her father's work.)

Knowing that Jack had sometimes signed his letters "Jackie Kerracky," I took to calling Jan "Janny Kerracky." She started to sign her cards and letters to me that way, and seemed to enjoy a funny nickname that didn't scream I AM THE DAUGHTER OF A LITERARY LEGEND. She sure was a loyal correspondent, although by this time her kidney failure had caused her eyesight to begin fading, and she relied mainly on tapes. And photos, lots of photos—Jan, Jan, the camera ham.

My second and final encounter with her occurred in February 1996, when she flew out to L.A. for a few days. She wanted to be in Santa Monica, near the ocean, breathing the sea air and listening to the waves crash. The doctors had warned her sternly against making the trip, saying it could kill her, but she came anyway. We went out to eat a number of times, once at Neptune's Net, the funky surfer/biker fish joint at the Ventura County line. She showed me where she'd lived in the seventies, on a hill near the Hollywood Bowl, and I showed her the old TV studio on Vine Street where her Dad had read excerpts from *On the Road* to Steve Allen's piano accompaniment.

Between the San Francisco benefit and this trip to Los Angeles, Jan had been told by her doctors that her health was too fragile for her to undergo the kidney transplant she'd hoped for. If she survived the surgery, the chances of rejecting the organ itself were too high. Jan took this philosophically and expressed a wish to move to Hawaii for the rest of her life—of whatever length and quality that life might be. "They have these turquoise pools," she told me, describing naturally-occurring ponds of paradise that shone like abalone shells.

She never did make it to Hawaii, but she did make a trip to Florida shortly after the L.A. trip, to give a deposition in her lawsuit alleging that the signature on her grandmother's will had been forged. Another plane, to another ocean, which is what she raved about when she called me from St. Pete Beach. "Lee, you oughta see how white the sand is here!"—a remark far removed from the unpleasant litigation that led her there.

Jan's writing is exhilarating, much of it more durable than her Pa's. In what Kerouac fans may consider blasphemy, I prefer Jan's impressionistic style to the monumentalism of *The Town and the City* or the tired alky voice of *Big Sur* and everything after it.

Perhaps Jan's only accomplishment to compete with the genius of *Visions of Gerard, Dr. Sax, On the Road,* or *Visions of Cody*—if you want to pursue this dumb idea of competition at all—was the way she lived. She traveled more extensively than her father, and her restless road lacked the safety valve of returning to the starched white clean Catholic order of "Memere." (In a cartoon published a few years ago in the *L.A. Weekly*, our beat hero says, "Iron my pants, I'm off to have adventures with Neal Cassady.")

Another principal difference is that Jan wanted to live. Jack had told John Clellon Holmes in the early sixties, "I intend to drink myself to death," and that's exactly what he did (in *Memory Babe*, Gerry describes his demise as "hemorrhaging esophageal varices, the classic drunkard's death"). Jan seemed to enjoy life and stopped her punishing drugging and drinking in time to forestall death. Until her kidneys failed in 1991, she retained the movie-star good looks she'd inherited from both her parents.

It's providential that Jan didn't live to see the heavily bowdlerized publication of her father's letters, and the sale of the original rolled manuscript of *On the Road* to a private collector for $2,430,000. Other countries, with official protection of their cultural heritage, would never stand for this shit. It's the equivalent of the British Museum selling one of the world's six Shakespeare autographs, or the Louvre selling the Mona Lisa.

Other than my slender file of Jan's letters and clippings and obits, there is one thing she gave me which I now treasure. In the spring of 1996, a parcel showed up at my front door, with the address written in familiar Janny-script. Inside was a hard plastic display box containing a heavy, die-cast metal model of a 1957 Chevy Bel Air. Except for the color, exactly the kind of car my parents bought soon after I was born, and the only kind of automobile to which I have any nostalgic attachment. Jan didn't know this—she'd just intuitively spotted it and the American Muscle designation on the box, and said it reminded her of me (blush). It didn't seem too important until it stared at me from a shelf in my garage, soon after Gerry phoned with news of Jan's death. As if I needed a more poignant reminder of picking up my first copy of *On the Road* when I was 16, dreaming of going 110 on a 2-lane road, listening to the radio station from Clint, Texas.

The ends of time are being tied as best they can. I had hoped the publication of Jan's unfinished *Parrot Fever* would tie up at least one of those loose ends, but that publication was mysteriously quashed even though the book was already listed on Amazon. Still, maybe we will get to read it someday. I hope the text doesn't conclude the same as Joyce's *Stephen Hero*, with a clammy "THE MANUSCRIPT ENDS HERE."

The great lady and her more famous father came and went entirely within the twentieth century. My memories of Janny Kerracky will never appear in an auction catalog.

Jan's last words before undergoing the fatal surgery, spoken to Lovelace Hospital social worker Diane Hebert, were: "Now I'll never be able to go in the water any more." But I have no doubt that she has found her turquoise pools.

John Allen Cassady

HOW I ALMOST MARRIED JAN KEROUAC

I first met Jan Kerouac at a Beat event at the old Spaghetti Factory restaurant on Green Street in North Beach, San Francisco. The event marked the ten-year anniversary of Jack Kerouac's death, and was also intended to publicize and celebrate the paperback publication of *Jack's Book* by Barry Gifford and Larry Lee. It was in October, 1979, and Jan and I were about the same age—in our mid 20s at that time.

I walked in and couldn't help but notice a strikingly pretty woman talking to a group of people. It was like one of those "across a crowded room" moments. She had laser-blue eyes and raven-black hair flowing past her shoulders over a very attractive figure. I grabbed the arm of someone nearby and asked, "Who is *that*?" "Why, that's Jan Kerouac. Have you two never met?" I was sure I would have remembered it if we had. "Come on, I'll introduce you," said my new friend, untangling his arm from my grasp. She was quite polite and shook my hand as she flashed a dazzling smile. I was tongue-tied for a moment, then blurted out a proposal of marriage, which was my wont in those days, but this time I was half serious.

"Think about it, Jan," I said with feeling, "it's a no-brainer! You're Jack's daughter—I'm Neal's son—and I'm sure they are looking down (sideways? up?) smiling in approval!" She looked a bit startled. "I mean, we're on a mission from God," I continued, borrowing a line from Dan Akroyd in the movie *The Blues Brothers*. "Think of our Beat progeny crawling around on the floor writing poetry!" She seemed unconvinced, and didn't exactly blow me off, but was obviously not taking me seriously. She offered some lame excuse like, "I'm going to South America to write, sorry." My hopes were dashed, but I heard later about what a tough life she had, starting with her father not acknowledging her as his daughter despite her spitting-image looks, so I had to forgive her. It was a sudden and spontaneous impulse on my part, I suppose, so who can blame her for politely declining the offer.

Some sixteen years later, author and friend Gerry Nicosia organized a benefit show at Fort Mason to help defer some of Jan's medical bills. Her failing kidneys required dialysis treatments four times a day, among other health problems she fought. All the "usual suspects," as I call them, were there to lend their voices in support, including Ken Kesey, Ramblin' Jack Elliott, Ken Babbs, and many more. There was a reception at the famous Enrico's restaurant on Broadway in North Beach beforehand, and I sat next to Jan for the obligatory photo opportunity for the local press. I hadn't seen her since that day at the Spaghetti Factory, and my first question to her was, "Do you remember me asking you to marry me that day?" To my surprise, she didn't, and seemed astonished that she couldn't recall such an event, even from that long ago. I was mortified to hear her say, "Are you kidding? I would have married you in a heartbeat!" Ouch!

The moral of the story: always ask them twice! Jan passed away not long after that, our last meeting, but I'm glad that at least I could meet her again and let her know how I felt about her, then and now.

By sheer coincidence, as I'm thinking of Jan, my sister Jami was cleaning out some bookshelves recently at her home in Capitola and came upon a copy of Jan's book *Trainsong*, published in 1988. In it was an inscription from her to me, which read, "To Johnny, Best Wishes, Jan Kerouac." Speaking of memory failures, I don't recall when or where she wrote that autograph, nor how it wound up in my sister's bookcase, so the mysteries of our lives continue.

Carl Macki

JAN KEROUAC — IN APPRECIATION

Maybe Jan Kerouac was a beautiful illusion. Her short life was filled with incredible experiences that moved me to pity and compassion, and I want to exorcize them from the collective memory of humankind. I have read enough by her and about her to want to read more by her. This is a fine start. My few times in her presence confirmed what the others have said about her. She was sweet, tough, impish, contrarian, and perhaps a bit of a demon to herself. I regret her passing, but the love and exuberance with which she looked out upon the world is still alive, just as it is with her great father. And the literary comparison to her father is about as striking as is her physical resemblance to him. That's what makes her a phantom in my mind. Perhaps the more she stays in print the more the reality of her life comes into better focus. God, I sure hope so.

I first met Jan at her apartment in Hollywood, in the mid Seventies, after getting her phone number from Kerouac biographer Gerald Nicosia. I had just blown in there, after taking a plane to San Francisco, and getting into some high jinks driving down California's fabled Route One. As I recall the first meeting, she was visiting with a friend, and sharing a joint. That was the only time I saw her use a drug recreationally. I immediately talked about writing with her, and pulled out a sheaf of manuscript, which somehow tumbled hilariously all over her floor. It was like a scene out of a Buster Keaton movie. So much for trying to

37

impress her with my suavity. Somehow I got in my mind that I should encourage her to write for *Wet* Magazine, a trendy Venice-based magazine at the time. She wasn't interested. She said she was determined to get her books out. Then I said, "Hey, I'm staying at the Westwood Hyatt, wanna go down there to drink?" But that was voted down for being too goddang highfalutin' uncomfortable.

My mother had just died, and what did I do with the money I inherited from her, but to start a long trek to California and down the Coast. And Los Angeles was my final stop in my quest for freedom from the hard winters of Chicago, a city which Beat poet Jack Micheline once remarked was "so corrupt it was actually honest." I found the shallowness of Hollywood to be actually refreshing, but was puzzled that Jan actually ended up there. I didn't ask her about that, but we talked some more. I was pretty full of it, and the joint only served to hype me up even more. Maybe to cut the chatter, or just shift the energy, after a while, Jan said, "Okay, let's go out." I took her to a Moroccan restaurant and bar just off the Sunset Strip. From the front windows of the place, we could see the Chateau Marmont, where John Belushi would die a few years later, and also where, earlier, if I am not mistaken, Janis Joplin made her final exit. There was an aura of eeriness to it. I don't think Jan liked me then. She certainly wasn't enraptured. The conversation went dismally. She wasn't hungry, and stirred her cocktail indifferently. We didn't stay long; it was a stupid place to go with her. I would have been much better off taking her to a natural foods restaurant.

Maybe at the time, I was too impressed by money. Jan was not impressed by material things—how could she be?—having experienced such hardship and struggles to survive in her early years. She was much more experienced than me about such matters. So was this a blown date? I didn't care; Jan was very attractive, and about three months younger than me, but I didn't feel that this could be a romantic relationship. I was not afraid of her, but what I heard about her past actually alarmed me. This coming from someone who was friends with junkies and prostitutes, and tried not to judge them. But Jan was a tragic figure, and the shadow of her father loomed over her rather than his light.

The next time I saw her was at a restaurant in Greek Town in Chicago, near the University of Illinois, Chicago campus. She was with Gerald Nicosia, with whom she was staying in Lyons, a suburb of Chicago. This time it was cool: I was broke, which she could dig. Jan scribbled poems on the bar napkins and we had a good time. We scribbled back and forth, as the bottle of retsina quickly emptied. I think Gerry picked up the tab. Jan noted that Greyhound bus stations were the Beat versions of Renaissance plazas. It all seemed to fit.

I remember the slogan from the Paris student revolts of the 1960s: "*Je suis Marxist, tendance Groucho.*" ("I am a Marxist of the Groucho variety.") That seemed to be completely apposite for Jan, even though she framed it in an aura of sweet sorrow.

One time she imitated my absent-minded, Brontosaurus-like clodhopping down Haight Street, which amused to no end my friend Albert Huerta, a University of San Francisco professor of Spanish literature. I had arranged for her to do a promo for a literature and arts program that was running on the radio at the time. The fact that hardly anyone listened to it didn't matter to Jan. She did a fine job, and we gave her and her boyfriend a room in a hotel on Haight Street for the weekend. Later, I heard she wrote about the trip to San Francisco and her parody of me in her diary, but I have yet to see it.

The last few times I saw her were in Marin County, and always at the Nicosia household in Corte Madera, a few heartbeats north of San Francisco. It appeared that she and Gerry were getting along rather well, and I saw no traces of any disenchantment with him by her, nor did Gerry seem to be anywhere close to the Svengali-like character some of his detractors were painting him as. She was on heavy dialysis, and seemed to be wrapped up in legal difficulties. I didn't know what to make of the dispute over her grandmother's will. I did talk to an attorney friend about the contest over the will, and he suggested that she file in Federal District Court in San Francisco for strategic reasons, the San Francisco region being more liberal than the rest of the country's Judicial Districts. I passed this on to Gerry, but I don't know if he even discussed it with her. At any event, I had no way to decide on the will. I heard that the alleged witness to the signing of the will later denied seeing any such thing, but it happened a long time ago, and I wondered whether a judge would even reopen the case. But the case seemed to be really wearing her down. At that time, she was receiving a fine share of the royalties from her father's books still in print. I think even now, *On the Road* alone sells more than a quarter million copies per year. For the first time, she had more than enough money, but she wasn't into that. However, she did have a financial adviser, and a coterie of new friends, attracted to her newly-won independence from money woes. Little did I realize the bonanza that the Kerouac Estate would become, and now wonder how she would have fared, during the Kerouac "money grab," had not her body given out on her.

And her death, well, her voyage home perhaps serves us well in these pages. The world was never a place where she seemed to be at ease. Doesn't that sound so saint-like? Once I was in discussion about some movie with her and Gerry, and used the adjective *mercurial*, and Jan asked me to repeat the word, so she could visualize it, get mesmerized by it, see it spinning like a tiny orb around her head like some planetary halo. That's how I'd like to remember her: a guardian angel of the written word—Saint Jan.

"Be crazy dumbsaint of the mind," said her father.

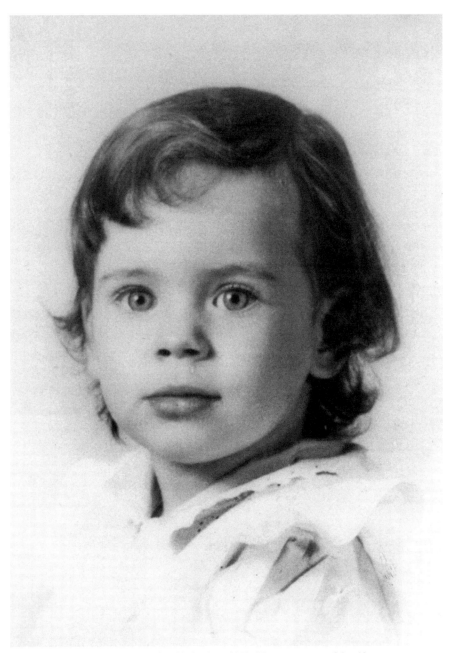

Jan Kerouac, Albany, New York, circa 1953. Photo courtesy of Jan Kerouac.

Jan Kerouac, Wappinger's Falls, New York, circa 1956. Photo courtesy of Jan Kerouac.

Jan with half-sisters Sharon and Kathy, Missouri, circa 1958. Photo courtesy of Jan Kerouac.

Jan in vamp makeup, Lower East Side, New York City, 1965, at a time when she was working as a 13-year-old prostitute. Photo courtesy of George Montgomery.

Jan in Los Angeles, July, 1978. Photo by Marie-Andrée Cossette.

Gerald Nicosia, Lil Dodson, and Jan Kerouac holding her omnipresent manila envelope marked "Everthreads," Huntington, New York, October, 1978. Photo by Stanley Twardowicz.

Jan baking one of her famous pies at Nicosia home, Lyons, Illlinois, June 1979. Photo by Gerald Nicosia.

Jan with Turkish ciga-rette and chocolate chip cheesecake, Sherlock's Home Pub, Chicago, June 1979. Photo by Gerald Nicosia.

Below:
Jan eating Czech svičkova, Old Prague restaurant, Ci-cero, Illinois, June 1979. Photo by Gerald Nicosia

Jan introduced at Red Rose Banquet of the National Society of Arts & Letters, Ritz-Carlton Hotel, Chicago, June 2, 1979. Sylvia Nicosia at right. Photo by John Herweck.

Jan in front of dim sum restaurant, Clement Street, San Francisco, with her father's friend, Chinese actor and painter Victor Wong, October 1979. Photo by Gerald Nicosia.

Jan with poet Jack Micheline at Naropa University's 25th anniversary *On the Road* conference, Boulder, Colorado, July 1982. Carolyn Cassady at right. Photo by Gerald Nicosia.

Jan in Cabo San Lucas, Baja, Mexico, January 1983. Photo courtesy of Jacques Kirouac.

Jan with her literary agent and good friend Peter Livingston at the Frankfurt Book Fair, October, 1983. Photographer unknown.

Jan in one of her "tropical paradises," mid 1980's. Photographer unknown.

Phil Cousineau

THE MYTHIC JOURNEY OF JAN KEROUAC

In a word, reverie. Reverie is the unexpected, but revealing, word that came to mind when I recently reread Jan Kerouac's first two autobiographical novels, *Baby Driver* and *Trainsong*, and then immersed myself in her unfinished third novel, *Parrot Fever*. Not simply escape, nor ecstasy, but reverie, the state of consciousness that may be described as dreaming with our eyes open.

As I traversed the haunted dreamscape of Jan's books, what first struck me was her characters' yearning for oblivion. But slowly the frequency of her oneiric language began to cast its spell. Words such as *trance, delirium, sleep, levitate, daydreaming, hallucinating, haze, daze, magic, paradise,* and *watery dreamworld* began to form another and subtler pattern. I saw her enchanted way of writing as more than a literary conceit. Instead, it appeared to be a valiant attempt to comprehend the frequently nightmarish realities of her life by plunging as deeply as possible into it, and hoping to come out the other side a little wiser. If her writing is an accurate guide to this journey, she spent her life seeking every imaginable form of reverie—on the road, in the bar, and over the typewriter. The pressing question for her was which aspect of reverie to choose from—creative, destructive, or some combustible combination of the two.

The work of the French philosopher Gaston Bachelard is enormously useful for understanding the mysterious relationship between dream, reverie, and the creative life. In his book, *The Poetics of Reverie*, Bachelard says that one has not truly seen the world until one has dreamed what one has looked at. This reflects an ancient worldview, one envisioned by the Dreamtime painters of Australia, evoked by Shakespeare, who wrote, "Our truest life is when we are in dream awake," and revered by Emily Dickinson: "Revery alone will do, / If bees are few." But Bachelard goes one step further by suggesting that we are actually created—and limited—by the strength of our reveries. "In our childhood," he writes, "reverie gave us freedom ... Psychologically speaking, it is in reverie that we are free beings ... This beauty within us is at the bottom of memory. It is the beauty of a flight, which revives us."

No doubt Jan Kerouac thought that flight was beautiful and revivifying as she winged her way around the world. But Bachelard is referring to an even more profound movement, the stirrings in the soul that reveal one's very depths. When she commented to her friend Brenda Knight that writing on napkins in lowdown bars and funky truckstops "barely preserved my sanity," she was confessing that her flights of fancy—her "precious reveries"—helped salvage some meaning out of the life she often feared she was wasting. Her ardent hope was that by paying close attention to her "infinity flashes from childhood," she might transmute the bizarre characters and byzantine plots of her life into literature—and maybe even heal her broken heart.

THE FLIGHT OF THE IMAGINATION

During the classical era of ancient Greece, Plato wrote that genius was not without a touch of madness. The theory of "Platonic madness" was revived in the Florentine Renaissance in the form of the popular belief that artists were "born under the sign of Saturn," the planet of melancholics. Philosophers described the temperament of the painters, sculptors, and poets of their era as contemplative, solitudinous, and obsessive, but also sinister, depressive and brooding. Eventually, their musings gave rise to the mythic image of the alienated artist. Three centuries later, in the Romantic era, notions about "sacred madness" and "divine enthusiasm" resurfaced in the lives of poets like Shelley, Keats, and Byron, who described his depression as a "Black Dog" that mercilessly hounded him. In modern times the belief that creativity is a bittersweet gift from the gods has been personified by innumerable novelists, poets, artists, and actors, ranging from Virginia Woolf, Anne Sexton, and Sylvia Plath, to James Dean, Jim Morrison, and Jan's legendary father, Jack Kerouac. Born under the same saturnine sign as these other moody artists, Jan's battles with creativity were intensified by her phantom father's reluctance to acknowledge her until she was in her teens.

Nevertheless, she was deeply affected by the almost gravitational force of his invisible presence. She spent half her life trying to replace him with adventurous and inaccessible men, or as she once described it, men that made her feel invisible. The other half was spent running home to the emotional sanctuary of her devoted mother, Joan Haverty—or its equivalent in the virtual paradises of hard drugs, remote islands, or communes. It is alternately exhilarating and exasperating to seesaw back and forth with her on these journeys between heaven and hell. What is finally so compelling is her desire to chronicle her descent into the underworld by being as brutally honest as possible.

Her first novel, *Baby Driver*, was a bluesy jaunt across the louche landscape of the Sixties, in which she vividly described her frenzied cross-country car trips as "reveries of swirling white lines." In this highly acclaimed work Jan's prose dazzled readers and critics alike, but as she later admitted to friends, she only occasionally scratched the surface of romantic self-destruction. Underneath the sheen of cool lurked a terrifying subterranean world of repressed feelings about her family, her tragic drug-addiction, and her violent relationships. Her second novel, *Trainsong*, delved deeper and sounded truer, as real as the moaning of the lonely freight trains that rode by her mother's home in Oregon. The book is suffused with her own distinctive brand of magical realism, as if she were the offspring of Jorge Borges and Frieda Kahlo. Despite the way the book wavered between pathos and bathos, incisive passages about her odyssey in search of her father, and a numbing list of seductions, conquests, and abuse, it held out the promise that the next book would round out her daring fictional self-portrait.

In the late 1980s, Jan began work on this, her third and final novel, as if it were the third act of an epic play. Soon after, she fell sick with the kidney failure that would take her life. The original title of the book, "Fired from Paradise," reflects the pessimism that shrouded her as the illness took its toll. The early drafts of the book mirror her doubts about ever finding—or deserving—the elusive Garden of Eden alluded at in the title. However, as her illness worsened, chinks appeared in her tough character armor. Through them a new light shone forth, and glints of optimism in her writing can be detected, especially in her plaintive expressions of happiness.

To convincingly complete the trilogy, Jan knew she had to somehow depict these two conflicting halves of her personality. Her innovative solution was the way she "twinned" herself into two half-sisters, Claire Haggerty (or sometimes Claire Luna) and Maxine LaCrosse. This literary legerdemain gave her the cool distance required of all true art. It also provided her with an opportunity to resolve, as with the focus of a camera, what she calls "the splintered vision" of her life. Claire and Maxine are the daughters of famous but absent fathers, a painter and writer, respectively. The novel describes them as incorrigibly romantic seekers looking for love and adventure in London, Puerto Rico, Greece, and finally Hawaii, the archetypal garden. But each time they think they have found their little piece of paradise they are "fired," which in the interwoven stories means being exiled by the law, frustrated by men, or banished by the fates. Never completely thwarted, Claire and Maxine turn to each other or their dying mother (modeled after Jan's mother, Joan) to learn what they need to about survival and the transformative power of love.

Significantly, the last chapter of the book is called "Apocalypso," a cleverly coined word from an incorrigible punster. The title captures the spirit of Claire's search for Maxine in the latter half of the book. While a reference to the biblical apocalypse would have conveyed anxiety about the calamities befalling the world, like the reference to the Chernobyl disaster mentioned in the book, the melding of "apocalypse" and "calypso" suggests a sultry dance performed while the world is coming to an end. Reassembled from fragments of her outline, taped commentary, and wildly strewn notes, the chapter serves as a fitting epilogue to her book and her life. Thinly veiled autobiography is a quicksilver mirror. But if the reader looks closely it is possible to imagine Jan herself dancing with her pen across the page right to the bittersweet end of her novel and her life.

"Jan Kerouac has written an exquisite allegory about the undiminished power of love in our crumbling world," wrote her close friend and her father's biographer, Gerry Nicosia, in his introduction to a chapbook version of this book, published in 1994. "Here are two sisters, or are they both halves of Jan's own fragmented psyche? As they play hide and seek with each other from country to country and city to city, is each merely chasing her own identity? And in loving each other, do they actually learn to love themselves (to fill the void of father-love they never had?) In the end, what matters is Jan Kerouac's own vision of what this life in the flesh should be, and not necessarily how it really is."

Jan's vision of what life might be is reflected in her revised title for the book, *Parrot Fever*. On the surface, the phrase refers to a rare disease transmitted by parrots, and which is alluded to at end of the story. But could she have been referring only to an arcane tropical disease? Or could she have been alluding to something more marvelous? As the Portuguese poet Fernando Pessoa wrote, "Everything is something else, besides." The clue that there may be something besides a medical problem came to me on the wings of a chance discovery. While poring over early drafts of the manuscripts, I found a fugitive line written in Jan's handwriting in the margins of the contents page that may reveal her more playful intentions: "Well, here I go again, and this time I've managed to catch parrot fever."

More than a throwaway line, the tantalizing image strikes me as a rhapsody on her father's Zen-inspired theme of "first thought, best thought" while writing poetry. "Parrot fever" sounds like one of her bebopping, riffing word-jags that endeared her to her friends. I find in it a feathered metaphor for the trajectory of Jan Kerouac's uncompromisingly independent life—the flamboyant flight and feverdream of the creative life, as well as the erratic nature of inspiration itself. The title change is vividly illustrated in the "parrot-sitting" sequences where she touchingly describes Claire's fascination with the "wild and uncaptured bird" that swoops around Jacob's apartment. It is a lovely image, but it also works metaphorically for the flights of freedom that were at the core of Jan's own self-image.

THE WRITER'S JOURNEY

The first time I saw Jan Kerouac was in 1979, in long shot, from the back of the sprawling, antique filled room of the venerable Old Spaghetti Factory in North Beach, San Francisco. I was there with a raft of friends to share in the celebrations for the tenth anniversary of her father's death. The raucous party was one of my first forays into the local literary scene. Recognizing Lawrence Ferlinghetti, Herb Caen, Ron Kovic, Herb Gold, Barry Gifford, and other hipsters, dandies, and cultural rebels, was a kick. But the highlight of the night for me was listening to Jan read from her father's work in a voice that carried faint traces of his French Canadian accent. After years of being outside the inside, as jazz musicians say, she was finally inside the inside. She relished her first taste of glory from being the daughter of the "King of the Beats," and seemed to dig, however temporarily, that her name and presence were catnip to the ardent fans who nuzzled around her, presumably to get as close to the mythic source as possible. She would later dismiss the attention as men trying to "touch her sacred flame."

It would be years before I saw her again. In 1995, at the Roxie Theater in the Mission District of San Francisco, I caught a special screening of John Antonelli's fine documentary, *Kerouac*, shown as part of a series of benefits for Jan's medical and legal bills. There was Jan again, but under the brunt of her illness, mellowed, humbled, even fragile. To the accompaniment of a funky bass player, she sang some soulful blues, a few old Motown hits in her best temptress voice, and even performed a credible Elvis impersonation. The crowd was full of black berets covering rapidly balding heads, neo-Beats clutching joints, and autograph hounds brandishing copies of *Howl, Gasoline,* and *Dharma Bums,* just in case one of the Beat royalty should appear.

After the wildly successful screening, a group of the usual poetic suspects were hanging out underneath the color-streaming neon marquee of the theater debating the virtues of the film, such as whether or not Antonelli had gotten the elusive "it" that is the soul force of Kerouac's work. The consensus was "as close as you can get in a film"; but while the debate raged on around her, Jan got restless and turned away to scope out the rest of the scene. Suddenly, she recognized a popular street character hovering in the shadows of the outdoor box office, an aging, gray-haired, ex-boxer named Ira Carter she had known 30 years before, in Greenwich Village. Gushing with pleasure like a young girl, she was evidently thrilled to see him, and asked if she could help him in any way. Later, she confided to friends with unusual tenderness that he was the man who had "taken my virginity."

In the summer of 1995, we met again at a dinner party at Gerry and Ellen Nicosia's home in Corte Madera, California, along with my companion, Jo Beaton, and John Antonelli. That night I was struck by the electric blue quality of her eyes throughout dinner, and later by the way her shoulders sagged as she emerged from the bathroom after her fourth dialysis treatment of the day.

After dinner, Gerry gently prodded her to talk about why she hadn't pursued her relationship with Jack. Wearily, she said that she knew from the time she was a little girl that he belonged to the world— not to her—and that it was her duty to protect him because he was so vulnerable. The challenge had always been, she told us, how to play the role of the daughter of a glamorous father without any help from him.

"He wasn't a great role model," she said, "so I had to hit the ground running." To her, that meant finding her own way in the world, and at the same time trying to carry on his legacy. "I'm not trying to imitate my father," she said, as if for the thousandth time, "I'm just try-ing to write in my own fashion ... Yeah, my dad was a genius—but I'm a genius, too!"

Although her illness had curtailed her physical movement, she made it clear that her mind was still racing when it came time to discuss writing. As scintillating as the dinner conversation was, what was most impressive to me was her passion she had for the writing life. As tea and coffee were served, Jan's eyes glazed as she stared off into the distance and said it was strange but necessary for her to work herself into a kind of altered reality in order to write. As Gerry told me later, the moment reminded him of the times he used to watch her sip her favorite honeyed tea in a café or slouch down in the backseat of a car, and actually see her spirit traveling out of her body. For him, that was the tell-tale sign that she was slipping into the deep, dreamlike attention she needed for her writing.

Wistfully, Jan went on to describe her determination to finish her book. But she was a woman of many determinations, also being com-mitted to fighting the good fight for her father's estate, and surviving the upcoming operation so she might someday find her own island paradise. Gerry mentioned to her that I had traveled to a few idyllic places around the world, like Polynesia, Bali, the Amazon, the West of Ireland, and Jan's eyes widened.

"Bali? Have you really been to Bali?" she asked, hopefully, as if looking for someone to give her the courage of her convictions to keep searching. I tried to paint word-pictures of the flickering tropical light, the daily ritual of taking fruits and flowers to the temples, and the old world kindness of the Balinese people. That's all it took for her to launch into her own riff about paradise, reaching for just the right *bon mot* to convey the life-affirming light on Maui. Finally, she simply said that the light there was so blindingly bright it seemed to have a streak of darkness in it. Her vision, she said, was of living out her life in a place with a turquoise pool. As she spoke, I got the distinct feeling she was trying to talk herself into returning there for good someday—if all went well with the kidney transplant she spoke ambivalently of getting. But it was also as if she saw everything through a film lens, as if her life had been a movie within a movie within a movie.

As we finished dessert, I thought of the way her father built a bridge of ecstatic words across the abyss between everyday life and the transcendent. But Jan chose her own way to bridge the rift in her life between darkness and light with irrepressible wordplay, friendship, and a penchant for showering people with gifts that rarely came her way.

Strangely moved by her almost preternatural loneliness as we were departing, I offered to visit her in Albuquerque, New Mexico, on my upcoming book tour that was planned for the following summer. She nodded wanly, and forced a smile that reminded me of a seen-it-all blues singer leaning against an old honky-tonk piano. Recalling that she was an omnivorous reader, I offered to bring along a few of my own books. Then it dawned on me that because of her fondness for literary trivia and word games (she used to spend three hours a day reading dictionaries or encyclopedias), she might especially get a kick out of my book of famous last words, *Deadlines*. So I offered up a sneak preview of the dying words of two of her favorite writers, James Joyce and Henry Miller: "Did nobody understand?" and "When am I going to get off of this carousel?"

Again, she laughed politely and said, sure, she'd love to look at my books and that I should actually send them to her so she could read them before I got to Albuquerque, which I did, but I never heard back from her. Her health kept deteriorating, and nine months later she was gone, dead of kidney failure, at the age of 44.

THE MYTHIC JOURNEY

Growing up in Detroit—Motown, the funky car capital of the world—during the 1960s meant mythologizing the road, either by hitting it or reading about it. Reading Mark Twain and John Steinbeck made you popular with your English teachers, but poring over Jack Kerouac's *On the Road* was practically mandatory with your roadster friends, like young Greeks growing up in fifth-century Athens dreaming of sailing across the wine-dark sea after reading a scroll of Homer's *Odyssey*.

Needless to say, a car-crazed, book-loving, blues-mad kid raised in a French-Catholic home with Canadian grandparents across the border in Windsor made me rather vulnerable to being influenced by *père* Kerouac. His work became the adrenaline shot I needed in my twenties to hit the road and drive across the "air-conditioned nightmare" of America (as Henry Miller had called it) in my bronze-colored '73 Capri, armed with pens, notebooks, a basketball, and jazz tapes. With Ray Charles' bluesy "Hit the Road, Jack" playing on my cassette player and Jack Kerouac's novels pored over in funky motels along Route 66, I came to believe that just maybe, somewhere down the road a piece, I, too, could reinvent myself. Which is why, nearly thirty years later, when the chance came to help out the man's daughter, it felt like the right thing to do.

With her passing, in 1996, the manuscript for *Parrot Fever* had languished in the archives. Finally, in the summer of 2001, I was asked by Thunder's Mouth Press to take on the task of editing, patching and reassembling the unfinished, scattered, but very promising manuscript. After my first look at the "monster in the box," as Spaulding Gray has called the early and unwieldy drafts of his novels, it felt like a daunting job. But I soon warmed to the challenge, thinking it would give me a rare opportunity to give something back to the universe, say thanks to someone who had profoundly influenced my life and work. But there's always something else, besides, as the poet said. In this case, it was the something I had never forgotten about my brief time with Jan: the razor-in-silk way she had pronounced the word *determined* when discussing her novel at that memorable dinner party in Marin County. "I'm determined to finish it," she had said, like a mountain climber, a long-distance bicycle rider, a painter going blind and racing against time. In retrospect, that word sounded to me like a lifeline she had thrown out into the world for someone to grab in case she needed help.

So I met with old friends of hers, including Gerry Nicosia, Brenda Knight, and R. B. Morris, and felt my determination to help in some way. Once I signed onto the project, I came to see that editing the book gave me an unusual glimpse into the creative process that I respect so much. Her way of imagining, her work ethic, her projected vision of the book, had all been frozen in time, caught in freeze-frame in the treasure trove of material left behind, which included rough drafts, interviews, outlines, letters, drawings, even screenplay and radioplay versions of the novel.

Reading through the pile of taped transcripts from her "talking reflections," it became apparent that she knew she might not survive the last operation. Near the end of her life, she spent hours in the solitude of her apartment talking on tape about her plans to finish the book. This was partly due to her failing eyesight and numbness in her fingers making it difficult for her to type anymore, and partly this was her way of cultivating the reverie she needed to make the imaginative leaps the book called for. Moreover, what touched me most was how the transcripts reveal her ardent desire to write herself back to life.

On those tapes she spoke about the status of each chapter and described what needed to be done. For Chapter 7 she wrote: "I don't know if there's enough for a whole chapter... Harmonica Virgins, because it's a pun on Harmonic Convergence, which the crazy new-age astrologers really took seriously and Maxine and Scarlet make fun of." For Chapter 10 she confessed some confusion: "I wrote a bunch of stuff... but I don't know where it went..." In the files for later insertions I found the lovely line: "My parrot's wings are green as her bosom," and advice from an astrologer to Claire "that the sun was rising in Greece when she was born, and therefore, if she were to live in Greece the sun would be rising in her soul every moment." A brief "Outline in Cinemascope" and a "Radio Play" version of *Parrot Fever* exposed Jan's filmic eye and her uncanny ear for sound. A final random page revealed her resolve: "New Year's Resolutions for 1991: 1) Finish Parrot Fever 2) Go to Puerto Rico 3) Get Healthy."

It was true, as Nicosia had once remarked to me: "A glamorous tragedy shadows the book." In my own reading of the work I found not your penny-novel confessional tragedy, but a mythic journey from light to dark and back again. As may be expected from a woman who read great literature throughout her life, mythic references pervade Jan Kerouac's work. In her books and in her conversation, she cites modern mythotragic characters like Billie Holiday, whose songs she loved to sing, Edith Piaf, who also claimed to regret nothing, along with dramatic references to John F. Kennedy, Marilyn Monroe, and doomed astronauts. But she also refers to several ancient figures such as Ariadne, Leto and Penelope, and many gods and goddesses of the underworld and the depths of the sea. Netherworld references are copious. She describes the deep fear of returning to "a parallel Hell," "scenes from the river Styx," "subterranean dungeons," "plutonian goodbyes," and "the den of Neptune." So it came as no surprise to me when Brenda Knight, one of Jan's closest friends at the end of her life, confirmed my hunch over lunch one day in Berkeley that Jan did indeed identify with the Greek myths, one in particular, Persephone.

One day the young Persephone was playing in a grove, gathering flowers, when she came upon a single scarlet poppy, which she innocently picked. Suddenly the earth split asunder and Hades emerged from the crevice on his chariot. The Roman poet Ovid writes that the moment Hades saw the lovely Persephone he felt a "rush of love" and seized her, then spirited her away down to his underworld kingdom. Forever after she was fated to spend half the year, the fall and winter, with the fearsome god of death as his captive bride, and the other half, the spring and summer, with her beloved mother, Demeter, up above in the warm world of light.

Consider the tantalizing parallels. Like Persephone, Jan's youth was torn asunder. In the sixties her heralded father was one of the most visible writers in the country, but he was virtually invisible to her. Fortunately, her mother was unquestionably devoted to her, unwavering in her love, but the damage had been done.

Out of this life of split loyalties, Jan too came to be known as the "queen of the underworld" and "princess of the demimonde." Over the years, descriptions of her varied so radically they suggested two different women. On the one hand, she was considered to be "schizophrenic," "tortured," "distant" and "cold," and on the other, "warm," "funny," "passionate," "full of vibrancy," "heartbreakingly vulnerable," and a woman with "brains and beauty and sensitivity." She was someone who would tenderly care for a friend's uncared-for plants, and shortly afterwards bluntly boast that her destiny was to be "pulverized, reduced to dust, to nothing," as she once confided to Gerry Nicosia.

If the contradictions seem to cancel each other out, maybe that was the desire. This soul-scorching desire is echoed in *Trainsong*, where she wails like the blues singer, "I had always dreamed of being able to make myself invisible."

SHEER SYNCHRONICITY

One afternoon, in the ill-fated fall of 2001, I met with Gerry in a café in Larkspur to review some issues about the manuscript. The air crackled with autumn crispness. The leaves on the trees around us were falling onto the stone terrace. The conversation of the other customers was hushed, mostly sorrowful discussions about the recent terrorist attacks. At one point during our meeting, I expressed my admiration for Jan's tenacity, the way she managed to keep writing day after day, despite enduring her dialysis treatment four times a day. "How did she keep going? Surely, she had to get discouraged, just like the rest of us."

Gerry smiled and said, "I think I know what helped get her through her writing block. One morning she called me on the telephone all excited and told me that the night before she had been channel surfing on her television and stopped when she found a documentary about the screenwriter, Waldo Salt, who wrote *Midnight Cowboy* and *Coming Home*, two of her favorite movies. She said the guy was so charming and humble about his down-and-out days in Hollywood that she was inspired to get back to her own writing. I'd known about him for years through his movies, but I had no idea that he had made a big impression on Jan. The thing about him that got to her was the way he introduced himself, not as an Oscar-winner, but as the writer of a few of the biggest turkeys of all-time. She loved that."

Before he could even finish his story, I was clapping my hands in sheer joy at the synchronicity that was unfolding. Not only did I know the documentary he was referring to, but through a marvelous co-incidence I was the sound man for the very interview that had captured Jan's attention. The film was *Waldo Salt: A Screenwriter's Journey*, an Academy Award-nominated documentary, and the sequence that Gerry had mentioned had been taped at the 1984 Mill Valley Film Festival where I had been one of the moderators for the panel discussions. As the screenwriting panel began, with Waldo, Paul Schraeder, Rob Nilson, Ann Richards, and others, I was asked by the festival videographer, Greg Gregory, to help him with the sound recording. I quickly agreed and got wired just in time to catch one of the greatest and most disarming introductions of all time: "Hello, my name is Waldo Salt, and I have written three of the worst films of all time." He didn't have to mention his 3 screenwriting Oscars; everyone in the audience knew that already. What he knew they didn't know was the constructive role that failure had played in his life, including his being blacklisted in Hollywood during the fifties, and how he had used the dark-night-of-the -soul portion of his journey to his advantage.

"If he could do it, I could do it," Jan said with great resolve after seeing the film. Soon after, she went back to work on her novel.

For years, I have used clips from that interview in my own film classes to illustrate the parallels between the classic hero's journey, the journey in drama, and the journey of everyday life. I have always introduced it as evidence of true humility, persistence, devotion to craft, and commitment to storytelling. Apparently, the same qualities moved Jan's heart enough to get her back to the typewriter. Learning of this serendipitous connection between us was one of those sly winks of fate from the gods that my commitment to the project was the right thing to do.

The year that has passed since that meeting has been tumultuous. The world seems to have irrevocably changed. But some things seem permanent, like the beauty of the city that I am looking down upon this afternoon from my lounge chair on the roof of our house in North Beach. I gaze through the wispy fog down the hill and see the same rabbit warren of streets where Jan's father used to wander, wine bottle in hand, spiral notebook in pocket, riprapping spontaneous poetry with Cassady, Ginsberg, and Corso, during the neighborhood's much-mythologized bohemian period. Thinking of them reminds me of one of Jan's fondest dreams, to someday "come home" to North Beach and open a restaurant called Chez Kerouac. If I close my eyes I can see her flipping Breton crepes and pouring hard cider for hardy souls on literary pilgrimages, in search of assurance that there is still a jazzy beat to this fair land.

While exulting in my own reverie about Jan and her many-splendored dream life, a flock of squawking parrots flies directly over-head, then swoops down the hillside and over the ghosts of the gold miners, the Beats, the Rat Pack, and immigrant ballplayers. It occurs to me that our neighborhood has recently caught its own strain of "parrot fever," having adopted them as ours after whoever had smuggled them in from South America had left them behind. Their rainbowed flights over the treetops in Washington Square Park, accompanied by their syn-copated aerial music, is now part of the daily feverdream of old North Beach.

While watching the parrots ride the light and sky-surf the bay breezes, I recall Jan's half-brother David mourning how she was always "letting the wind blow her" every which way, not unlike the parrots in the sky above me. But I see her flights of imagination as acts of will to move herself beyond the repressive bourgeois life and stifling confor-mity that were the bane of her life, but also towards something far more remarkable. Bachelard called it the revival of the imagination. In this sense, the fever that is reprised at the end of the book can refer to more than disease. It may be seen as an example of the *double entendres* she loved to lay on her friends and readers, an improvised image flaming forth out of her fiery soul to describe the way her temperature soared when she willed herself into reverie so she might write herself back to life.

As her last novel shows, beyond the burnished image of her vaunted family name that preceded her everywhere she went, Jan glowed with her own gently fading beauty, and wore well her aura of tragic bravado.

North Beach, San Francisco, October, 2002

Jacques Kirouac

JAN KEROUAC'S FRENCH-CANADIAN FAMILY

Early in the fall of 1988, I heard that Jan Kerouac, the only child of the Franco-American writer Jack Kerouac, would come to Quebec City and that I could meet her. At that time, she was completely unknown to me. So I started reading *Baby Driver*, her first novel.

I must say that, after finishing the whole book, I had a rather negative opinion about her and said to myself : *What kind of girl am I going to meet during the cocktail party given in her honor at the Secrétariat Permanent des Peuples Francophones?* This cultural organization was located in the lower town of the old city of Quebec. At that time, I was the president of L'Association des Familles Kirouac (the Association of Kerouac Families), and if I was very interested in Jack Kerouac as a writer, I had no interest in his daughter and even her books. When I saw her for the first time, she was quite far from me, moving around some people. I could see she had a nice smile and was well dressed in a skirt.

After a few minutes, I met her, and I was immediately struck by her blue eyes, which were so shining that they looked like crystal. She was quiet and looked serene, and when shaking my hand, she said a few words in a very understandable English because she was speaking slowly with a complete articulation of the words. My negative apprehension had vanished, but the best was still to come.

In fact, I invited her to dinner with the members of the board of directors of our Family Association. So the day after, I was at her side for at least two hours. During all that time, she was like an open book, telling me many parts of her life, but mainly about her only two meetings with her father. She was sorry not to have any souvenir from him except a cork of a bottle of wine from when she met him for the first time. She did not eat very much and took no wine, telling me she had given up drinking.

She told me she was living like a monk in her flat in Kingston, New York. During that meal, she made some sketches and drew a car on the white placemat that was on the tablecloth. She did all that with much simplicity, smiling all the time, but almost never laughing. She never spoke loud, being coy (or reserved) all the time.

So, at the end of our meal, I had a completely different point of view on her life and on herself. I must say that from that very moment, we became friends for good till the end of her life. After two hours of discussion, she told me she felt tired; but before leaving the group, she made a short speech. She told us she was happy to find a new family with our Family Association, of which she became a regular member.

By the end of our first meeting, I was impressed by her great simplicity. She was without any pretensions, and I felt very affectionate toward her. To me she was not responsible for the poor childhood she had had because of the absence of her father.

A few months after our first meeting, she sent a short article for our family newsletter *Le Tresor des Kirouac* about her trip to Quebec. Here is one except:

"When we got out of the car, the very first thing I saw was the apparition of Chateau Frontenac. I didn't even know about it yet, but the eerie underlit spires seemed to broadcast its name right into my head. Then we trudged up the street, where I was amazed to find a brass placard riveted to the side of a stone building with *Club Jack Kerouac* engraved in it right at eye level. Suddenly I remembered how I used to look through the monstrous Manhattan phone book as a child in New York City searching in vain for my name and finally came to the reluctant conclusion that I was some kind of freak.

"Well, not here, I'm not. Hey! This is my kind of town. Upstairs in an enormous room I met a great collection of people, all very warm and *simpatique*. And in the midst of them all were two sky blue eyes beaming at me like a beacon of recognition... My cousin Jacques Kirouac, the President of the Association. When I met him and held his hand, I instantly felt a bond much closer than I feel to my grandmother or my uncle! Looking into Jacques' eyes, I felt as if I were staring into a mirror."

As one may see, we were in a good mood from that moment, and we kept on friendly terms with each other. Although we were not closely related, I became the closest Kirouac to her, and some years afterward she told me that I was a kind of uncle for her. So, some months later, in March 1989, I stopped at her flat in Kingston, New York, while driving to Florida with my wife. She was living in the historical part of the city. Big trees almost hid the stony houses. But her flat was located in a rather old house which needed to be refurbished. She was waiting for us on the porch to be sure we would find her. Once inside, I was surprised not to find much furniture. She had almost nothing, and she told me that the things I saw did not belong to her. She was really poor, having only a mattress right on the floor in the middle of an empty room.

I saw she was working on a book that she would later call *Parrot Fever*, but at that moment it was still entitled *Fired from Paradise*. With much simplicity, she then told me that her books were her children. Looking sad, she glanced at a stack of books on the floor. She told me those books were written by her father, but that she had not read them all. That surprised me a bit, but I did not ask why.

In another room, I was surprised to see the Quebec flag hanging on the wall. Some years later, she told me she was in favor of Quebec sovereignty. I did not think that she was interested in that question, but, in the long run, I found she was very concerned about her roots.

Almost at the end of our meeting, we went to a small room, where there was absolutely nothing but papers and boxes on the floor. Amongst that mess, she was looking for pictures, and she gave me a wonderful one taken in a boat on the west coast of the United States. Though she had almost nothing, she offered me a full loaf of bread that she had baked. It was too much for me, especially knowing she had so little food. So I took only half of it, but I was really impressed by that gift, which showed how important it was for Jan to share with others.

I left her with the promise to see her in Florida later on; but when she went to Sarasota, I was only able to get her on the phone. That was our first missed rendezvous. I understood later on that she was like a bird flying from tree to tree. It was not easy to catch her. The same event occurred during the following summer when she wanted to come back to Quebec in order to visit Riviere-du-Loup, the land of her grandfather. To make plans, even on the spur of the moment, was not very easy to do with her.

But we kept in touch mainly through postcard. I was amazed by her choice of them: very colorful, funny subjects, very short texts with drawings, stamps overlapping, red ink, etc. So to me that appeared to be a little bit original, not to say eccentric, but I was always glad to read them because I was receiving her feeling at that moment.

Then after that period of time, she wrote me she was going back to Eugene, Oregon, to take care of her mother, who was dying from cancer. So I lost track of her for quite a while, not even knowing she had been in Puerto Rico, where she almost died from kidney failure. So I was very glad to hear her on the phone from her new home in Albuquerque. Of course we talked about her sickness, but we now had another subject to talk about: the Sampas family! She was arguing that her grandmother Gabrielle's signature on her testament was a forgery, and she wanted to sue the Sampases. But being sick, she relied on her friend Gerry Nicosia and wanted our Family Association to give her moral support.

Some time after that, she phoned me again asking me to meet her in New York City in order to help her in her lawsuit against the Sampas family. I had been reluctant to go there, unsure of what I could do to help her, but after a phone call from Gerry Nicosia, I changed my mind and went to New York at the beginning of June, 1995. It would be the third time I saw her and also the last.

In fact, I met her in the lobby of her hotel near Times Square. Right away I saw a difference in the way she looked, compared to that previous time some years ago. Her skin was no longer smooth and youthful, being darker and having the appearance of parchment. Her blue eyes, although still glossy, had some jaundice in the white part. She was almost skinny. She appeared to be unwell, if not actually gravely ill. After some discussion in her room, I left her with her friend Gerry Nicosia. We both agreed that she was quite vulnerable, partly on account of the four dialyses a day she had to make and all the medicines that went with that. I felt sorry to see her that way, and Gerry and I agreed to take good care of her. The day after, walking the streets, I noticed another problem: she had trouble with her equilibrium, so she had to have someone hold her arm.

It would take too long to make a complete account of the four days while we were together. I only will recall some facts which are related to the main concerns Jan had at that moment: her lawsuit against the Sampases, to save the legacy of her father's literary heritage. I soon found out that she came to New York to take part in the Symposium on Jack Kerouac mainly for that reason, seeing it as a unique chance to prevail against that Sampas family and win her rights to her father's estate.

I saw her giving a press conference in front of the conference hall, near Washington Square. Very quietly and not raising her voice, she gave her point of view on the quest to save Jack's papers. After answering some questions, she then concluded, saying: "I leave the rest to Gerry Nicosia, because I am too sick to keep talking."

Another day, on the sidewalk facing Town Hall with a group of demonstrators backing her cause, she acted as a "cheerleader." I was surprised to see her almost jumping with a placard that had "KEROUAC GATE" written on it. And she was shouting in a loud voice. To me, she appeared to be at least twenty years younger, and I was at the same time happy to see her with that youthful demonstration and sad because I knew her energy was only temporary. After that, we went to a restaurant, where she ate less than half the food she had been served. She was exhausted and left again for a dialysis.

In fact, she was not very well during all the time she was in New York, having also a sore on her foot that was very painful. In spite of all that, she wanted to make a short speech at the opening of the symposium on her father at New York University. I was at her side when she stood up to walk toward the stage, intending to speak at the microphone. Her "godfather" Allen Ginsberg was the master of ceremonies. Unfortunately, nervous and frail as she was, she didn't reach the narrow staircase to the stage until her way was already blocked by the program director of NYU, Helen Kelly. Then the police escorted her and myself outside the hall to the sidewalk. We were very disappointed, and the press conference was given outside. I must say that one of the panelists came to tell me that he was in favor of Jan but that he could not express his point of view in public! Jan was apparently bothering many of the university administrators, who made it clear that she was not welcome.

In spite of her illness and the stress due to the struggle to save Jack's papers, Jan did not forget the hard years of her childhood she had lived not far from Washington Square Park, where we took a walk alone together. Sitting on a bench, her purse fell to the ground, and almost all the contents scattered all around, including her money. So I stood up to pick up all the money. Then she told me: "Jacques, leave that there for the poor." Sitting back down on the bench, she told me that while living on the Lower East Side of Manhattan, she would walk barefoot on the sidewalks trying to find some food in the garbage cans. She also told me she would steal money from the poor box to feed herself, and she offered to show me the church where she had done this. She told me all these things without any bitterness.

When I left her after our time together in New York, she said she planned to move from Albuquerque, New Mexico, to San Francisco. But after some problems in northern California that summer, she went back to Albuquerque. All during that period from the conference in New York to her last stay in Albuquerque, we kept in touch almost once a month mainly through phone calls rather than post cards. I saw her health was far from improving. We talked about the difficulty she had finishing *Parrot Fever* on account of her visual problems. But her main concern was her lawsuit against the Sampases. That was draining all her energy and putting much stress on her life. So there was not very much time left for that third book, even if to my mind she knew exactly what was to be written.

Still, during that period of her life she sent to me a very moving letter that is still unpublished. Like her father in *Visions of Gerard,* she evokes what was then thought to be our family motto when she writes:

"I now understand fully the Kerouac Family motto: AIMER, TRAVAILLER et SOUFFRIR. I love my father, work on my book and suffer endlessly with health problems." First she applies the family motto to herself. Her first love, she said, went to her father, whom she had been searching for her whole life. Her work was writing, and at that moment, she was working on *Parrot Fever*. But due to severe illness, she could not complete that book, which would conclude the trilogy. It's interesting to note that Jan, like her father, was evoking suffering not only as an intellectual topic but also as a personal matter. She refers to her family motto to point out her ties with the Kerouacs the same way her father had used that same family motto to connect with his Breton origins. A little bit further, in concluding, she writes:

"I hope you wonderful people of Les Familles Kerouac will take up the fight to preserve our honor because I am now too weak to fight anymore."

That letter was written on August 17, 1995, less that a year before her death. Her health was still deteriorating, but she wanted to keep on with the lawsuit against the Sampases. She appreciated the moral stand of our Family Association, which she considered her own family, but the effective work on the ground was done by Gerry Nicosia, whom she valued as the only one to help her in the United States. In Jan's mind, the lawsuit was more than strictly personal, for she wrote that it concerned "our honor." Jack's only daughter felt almost alone at the end of her life, but she relied on the Kerouac Family Association to help her. It is significant that in the United States the badge with our crest became the sign to identify Jan's friends. Jan on her personal card had a fleur-de-lis, symbol of her French roots. I saw that Jan, at the end of her life, was getting closer to her genuine family, so it was not surprising, but rather meaningful, that she wanted to be buried in the Kerouac family plot in Nashua, New Hampshire, even though she never lived in that place.

I got her last postcard in April, 1996. She mainly wrote me that she was tired from the lawsuit and from all the delays caused by the Sampases. But in spite of all that, she planned a trip to Lowell in the coming fall.

At the end of May, I got her last phone call; it was nine days before her death. She was coming out of the hospital but going to a nursing home on account of her illness. She told me she was now sure she was Jack's daughter because of her blood disease. But she was confident of getting better, because she intended to go to St. Petersburg, Florida, with her ex-sister-in-law Deborah Bower for the lawsuit against the Sampases to save Jack's papers. She told me she was no longer able to travel alone. There was not a single word on her third book.

At the end of that call, she told me she would send me her picture with the flowers I had sent her at the hospital. Instead, I got a phone call from Deborah Bower in early June telling me that "Jan has passed away last night." I was crushed by this news, and even six years after her death, I am still moved just by writing those lines. In fact, I was saddened by the entire end of her life, when she was fighting strongly to save Jack's papers. She really suffered from the opposition of the Sampas family, who controlled her father's estate. If her first two books were mostly autobiography, the third one was different and more difficult to produce, and it would prove too much for Jan, who told me in New York that she knew she was to die in the next few years. So she left us with an incomplete work but one that is more analytical of her own life, as I found out in reading some published excerpts from *Parrot Fever* she gave me in New York on June 3, 1995. That was my birthday.

Mary Emmerick

JAN KEROUAC: A SPONTANEOUS LIFE

People have spoken of Jan Kerouac writing like her father Jack but from a "female perspective." For me, Jan's so-called female perspective was really a wonderful sarcasm. Her lines "And what demonically divine providence had led me to Malcolm ... my life had evidently been too easy so far, and the powers that be were shifting the balance by steering me into this man" were heavily underlined in my copy of *Trainsong*. I still have "Malcolm stories" I'd like to share with her, like the one about the guy I lived with in Greenwich Village in the late 50's who painted an occasional watercolor and sold it in the Village bars while having a drink. On weekends, in-season, he went to Northport with some other "clam diggers" to dig. Often they ended up at Jack Kerouac's house, and knowing how much I wanted to meet him, he'd come home and torture me with Kerouac stories: "Jack told the funniest story about sleeping all night in a church pew. In the morning some old lady came in and was kneeling praying, and he rose up from his pew, arms waving, and yelled, 'Whoo, I'm the Holy Ghost,' and the old lady keeled over," etc.

To my "Malcolm" he wasn't the author of *On The Road*; he was just another drunk telling stories. Why was I never invited? Hey, it was the 50's, and I wasn't a "clam digger." On one of his binges at Jack's, he "borrowed" someone's car, totaled it, and got six months on a work farm in upstate New York. (He'd never been in back of a wheel before.) But

75

by then, it was time for me to flee to San Francisco where I met most of the Beats, Ginsberg, Ferlinghetti, even Neal Cassady while working as a waitress at Vesuvio's next door to City Lights and living in the flat below Richard Brautigan before his fame and alcoholism. Then his beverage of choice was orange juice. Sitting alone, he'd order a glass every night in the Vesuvio. At closing time, he'd turn the glass upside down and leave me my biggest tip of the evening, 50 cents. I'd like to exchange Brautigan stories with Jan who met him in Amsterdam drinking himself sober.

Jack Kerouac always remained elusive. Instead, I met another Kerouac, Jan, who died on June 5,1996, one year to the day I saw her last, a day on which we had no time to talk about "Malcolms" or "Brautigans."

On June 5, 1995, at 10 A.M., we were being escorted by police from New York University, where Jack's friends were gathered for a conference called "The Writings of Jack Kerouac." Before we hit the pavement we heard Jan's godfather Allen Ginsberg's voice: "Good evening, ladies and gentlemen. Don't pay any attention to those people." That slip-of-the-tongue was the only evidence he gave that he was actually somewhat rattled by the affair.

Before continuing the events of that day, I'd like to go back to two earlier more carefree summer days. The first was July 30, 1982, in Boulder, Colorado. Jan and I were among 1200 attendees who had crossed the Americas and Europe to be at what Abbie Hoffman would dub "Camp Kerouac—the greatest class reunion in history." (Naropa Institute and Allen Ginsberg, who arranged it, called it a ten-day-festival to celebrate the 25th anniversary of the publication of *On The Road*.) People were sleeping everywhere from the landmark Boulderado Hotel to the Rocky Mountains and the County Jail. Many were from the classes of the 50's and 60's, but I saw a six month-old and a 68-year-old hobnobbing with the famous. (Picture Allen Ginsberg, Timothy Leary, Paul Krassner, Abbie Hoffman, and William Burroughs up on stage together with a painting of Jack--crucifix prominent--in the background, while the Grateful Dead stroll past below.) There were workshops, panels, readings, and even picnics, but mostly reunions of old friends and the making of new.

Jan had been living in Eugene, Oregon, baking bread when she received the invitation from her godfather and still "guardian angel"

Allen Ginsberg. At the time, I was surprised that she was not included on the "Kerouac and Women" panel composed of Joyce Johnson, Carolyn Cassady, Edie Kerouac Parker, Joanna McClure, Fernanda Pivano, and Joy Walsh. (Twenty years later, I am not surprised. It would have been difficult for them to excuse Jack's conduct as just a "50's thing" with Jan sitting among them.) Instead, perhaps as an afterthought, she read with Joyce Johnson, fresh from the Women's Panel, Peter Orlovsky, Ray Bremser, and Gregory Corso. Quiet, shy, barefooted, black hair streaming, she nervously began reading two selections from her mother Joan Haverty's work, which later appeared in Joan's posthumous book *Nobody's Wife*. In the first, Joan left Jack only to find him atop of his desk in the moving van when it arrived at her new apartment. For this she had to pay $10 extra. (In Jan's reading they had been living in a loft, but in the published account they were living with Jack's mother.) In the second, Jack tries to wheedle her into baking him a coffee-iced spice cake after Joan comes home from work exhausted. She refused and went to bed, but as always the more tired Memere comes in later from work or a union meeting and proves her greater love by sending the aroma of spice cake wafting to Joan's nostrils in the wee morning hours. Jan was to write a humorous song about it, "Spice Cake Rap," which she performed at the 1994 NYU Beat symposium.

In Boulder in 1982, she followed up with a few poems and dreams of her own. With Allen's assurance that she had plenty of time, she said, "I'll read from three [there were only two] of the meetings with my father," and then nervously spun into the often repeated excerpts from *Baby Driver*: the blood test to prove paternity when she was nine and his promise to "See ya in Janyary!"; and the visit to Lowell when she was 15, pregnant, and on her way to Mexico, when Jack tells her, "Go to Mexico, write a book, you can use my name." If the applause she received was only polite, she didn't notice. *Baby Driver* had just been published, but she wasn't looking for literary adulation. She said her goal was to find her father inside herself. She was just another class member, exuberant to be publicly performing with so many of her father's friends for the first time. They called her their "little princess," but none of them told her that she was entitled to half of the royalties on Jack's books. It was a stranger, John Steinbeck's son, who told her that.

I saw a different Jan on June 23, 1988, in Lowell for a five-day-affair culminating in the unveiling of The Jack Kerouac Commemorative, eight triangular columns inscribed with excerpts from ten of his books set in Eastern Canal Park. Vagueness, distance, and defiance had replaced Jan's shy exuberance. Sunglasses, hands on hips, she reluctantly posed for fan pictures. As of '85, she was finally getting a small, long overdue share of the royalties. Her second book, *Trainsong*, had been published, which she downplayed saying that she only received a $3,000 advance over five years; and she'd be lucky to repay it the way the agent and publisher were marketing the book. "You could make more money playing the Lottery," she said. Only five copies of her book had been sent to Prince's Bookstore, the leading Lowell bookseller. They sold instantly, and no more were available.

But her wanderlust hadn't changed. When Edie Parker Kerouac asked where she lived, she gleefully answered, "Nowhere." She'd come from Eugene via Greyhound. "I hate Eugene, but my mother's ill there. I stopped in New Orleans, then Manhattan, now Lowell, then I go back to apartment-sit in Brooklyn, then I want to buy a house near water, maybe Florida's Gulf Coast because I can't live without swimming every day."

The "Lowell Powers That Be" had ignored Jan completely, but Gerry Nicosia had urged Brad Parker of the Lowell Corporation for the Humanities to buy her a ticket to Lowell, since she was as usual broke at the time. Gerry was understandably concerned when he, his mom Sylvia, and I picked her up at the hotel to go to a reception and saw plate upon plate of "picked at" food. Gerry visualized huge room-service bills. Father "Spike" Morissette, her father's boyhood priest, ended up paying them. The "beatnik princess" was in the sixth year of her reign and scorned the "academia nuts," her father's fans, the wives Stella and Edie, and the Lowell politicos. "They owe me" was her attitude. She'd paid her dues from the Lower East Side to the shacks of Ellensburg, Washington. "Who's going to pay for the cab?" "I have no money," was her reply, to Gerry's consternation.

Richard Scott, who was director of the Lowell Heritage State Park, was having the reception at his mother's house for that evening's forum participants: John Tytell, Regina Weinreich, Ann Charters, and Robin Moore, author of *The Green Berets*, *The Happy Hooker*, and *The French Connection* and friend of Brad Parker, who was there along with Jan and Gerry and his mom. I got in through Gerry's good graces.

"There's always plenty to drink at these things," he said. "Mom and I want you to go, and we'll share our food." The reception was in a small Lowell home, where we met Richard's wife, mother, and seemingly half a dozen little white-haired-maiden aunts, for whom meeting so many "literary lights" had to be the event of a lifetime.

We sat in the living room and the "room-temperature cocktails" were tomato, orange or apple juice served on a white-doileyed tray by a smiling, aproned, white-haired lady, who was followed by yet another carrying the ice bucket. Both then disappeared. The usual buffet—shrimp, cheeses, etc.—was generous; and everyone was stuffed and ready to leave when the announcement came, "Dinner is served." Robin's wife Mary Olga, a relatively young, statuesque blonde wearing a designer dress and rose-colored shades, turned "green" as we looked in the dining room and saw a place set for everyone with their best china, lace tablecloth, and cloth napkins. Each lady stood bearing a huge platter: beef brisket, spare ribs ("we removed the bones so they'll be easier for you to handle"), cabbage, potatoes, beets, and various other hearty dishes. "You go ahead, Robin and I ate just before we came, and we'll wait for you in the living room," said Mary Olga. The aunts insisted they join us. Mary O. daintily nibbled a few shrimp she hastily brought from the buffet. Robin piled his plate over and over.

Meanwhile John Tytell was staring at Mary O. He finally asked, "Don't I know you from somewhere?" She looked surprised, a bit aghast. He finally snapped his fingers and said, "I've got it. Weren't you in *The Happy Hooker*?" Humorously she answered, "No, I was one of the Green Berets."

Jan let John be her warm-up act. Purposely looking Mary O. up-and-down she asked, "You got any kids?"

"No, I don't have any children."

"I don't blame you. I don't have any either. You can't sleep all day if you've got kids, can you? My father didn't want any either. He didn't want me. Only saw him twice. Once for the blood test to prove I was his even though my mother was married to him when I was conceived, and you don't find that often, do you?", etc., etc., until the announcement, "Dessert is served. Homemade apple pie and ice cream or strawberry shortcake with strawberries grown in the garden?" Mary O. declined.

And who but Jan would say, "If she doesn't want hers, give me two, one of each."

"Of course you can have two, Dear, but we have more than enough for everyone so she can have hers too."

I thought how sad Jack isn't here. If he stumbled around after those who are "mad to live, mad to talk ... desirous of everything at the same time," he needed to go no further than a mirror image seated in a modest residence in his beloved Lowell.

By June 5, 1995, Jan's body had failed her. She was on dialysis four times a day. She had repeated the recitation of the two Jack visits too often. So much that had been painful was unimportant that day, like the circulating photo of a handsome, shyly smiling Jack with Carolyn Cassady and her children Cathy and Jamie taken in 1952, the year Jan was born. Joan was now dead. So how could it matter that Carolyn Cassady told *Rolling Stone* that she was tired of people condemning Jack alone for Jan's self-destructive life, and perhaps her mother might have had some influence? Jack's 34th chorus of "Orlanda Blues" didn't matter: "The only responsibility to a child is to feed.... And the girl gets married? I have a bunch of stray cats in my yard... I wouldn't have a daughter." Jack had said the "KER" in their name meant house, and she never owned one by the water or anywhere else, but that didn't matter. It hurt deeply that she had to write a check for $120 to NYU to attend a conference called "The Writings of Jack Kerouac" honoring her father, and that her father's friends turned their backs because she was contesting her grandmother's will. But what mattered to Jan on June 5, 1995, was telling his friends how upset she was that Jack's work and personal effects were being sold piecemeal, and how important it was to sell the archives to a university, preferably the Bancroft in Berkeley, which had offered one million dollars.

With her godfather Allen chairing the first panel and other of her father's friends on the stage with him, like Ray Bremser, her reading partner from '82 in Boulder, and Anne Waldman who called her "our little princess," surely she'd be permitted to tell them. Jan, accompanied by an elderly gentleman from Quebec, Jacques Kirouac, founding President of l'Association des Familles Kirouac Inc. (Jack said his family was 5,000 years old), approached the stage. Simultaneously at the back of the auditorium, Bobby Waddell (a Vietnam vet Gerry wrote about in *Home To War*) and I unfurled a huge blue banner saying, "Save Jack's Papers." Instead of a cordial or at least civil welcome, the friends had her stopped by police like a common nuisance. It appeared as if they were going to arrest Gerry, who was yelling for Allen to let her come up on stage, so instead of a plea to save Jack's books a weeping Jan cried out, "Maybe they should arrest Gerry--then people would know what a travesty this gathering is--but I don't want him arrested because he's adopting a Chinese baby." (China permitted no adoptions from Americans with any kind of arrest record.) Bobby, the vet at the other end of the banner, called, "I'm not going to adopt a Chinese baby. Arrest me instead." I looked at him and under other circumstances it could have been a "Malcolm" moment. Instead, pushed along by the university police, we followed Jan, Gerry, and Jacques to the street.

Outside and still crying Jan ripped off her orange-and-white conference badge announcing THE WRITINGS OF JACK KEROUAC and underneath: JAN KEROUAC, NEW YORK UNIVERSITY. She threw it into the gutter debris. Also outside, a group of poets calling themselves The Unbearables were protesting the $120 fee and passing out xeroxed "Federal Reserve Notes" for $100 bearing Jack's and Neal's photos. One ran to pick up the badge, but another said, "Don't. Leave it there. Who knows who will find it? Maybe it will be put away for years and years and one day maybe...." And it was left there.

Later Jan's party of supporters, now joined by the Unbearables, positioned ourselves across from Town Hall, where the "luminaries" were having a reading and concert and being photographed by Annie Leibovitz. There we were joined by two young men fresh from a Francis Ford Coppola casting call for *On The Road*, who had auditioned for the roles of Jack and Neal. That evening our "beat" ragtag crew traveled to a cheapo restaurant in Times Square with "the would-be Neal Cassady" only briefly letting go of Jan's arm to dance in traffic and sing "Singin' in the Rain." We kept her out much too late, but as she entered her hotel room, "Neal's" parting words were, "All my life I wanted to meet Jan Kerouac," and she smiled.

I never saw Jan after that night, but as I read Todd Bauer's last interview with her for *Beat Scene* I think of his question, "How do you want to be remembered?" and her answer, "As the daughter who saved my father's archive from total destruction." I'd like to tell her she succeeded. When the manuscript for *On the Road* sold for 2.43 million dollars, and its new owner said he'd like to display it next to the Lombardi Trophy, emblematic of victory in the Super Bowl,

I thought of the words, "the whole world's watching." This was not the sale of a raincoat to Johnny Depp. The rest has to go to a library as Jan hoped. I hope I understood correctly that his remaining archive has been bought by the New York Public Library's Berg Collection (though Jan preferred the Bancroft). I also hope that her cousin Paul Blake Jr. receives his due share from the Sampas family, but that's another story. Right now I just think of Jan not having to wait any longer for the "Janyary" visit.

Jan with Jack Kerouac's boyhood priest, Fr. Armand "Spike" Morissette, holding *Memory Babe*, in Lowell, Massachusetts, for the dedication of the Jack Kerouac Commemorative, June 1988. Photo by Gerald Nicosia.

The dinner party in Lowell, June 1988, that Mary Emmerick describes in her memoir. Clockwise from blonde woman at front center: Mary Olga Moore, author Robin Moore, Kerouac scholar Regina Weinreich, Brad Parker, Lowell Heritage State Park Director Richard Scott, Jan Kerouac, Mary Emmerick, and Sylvia Nicosia. Photo by Gerald Nicosia.

Jan meets Jacques Kirouac at a party at the Secretariat Permanent des Peuples Francophones, Quebec City, December 1988. Photo courtesy of Jacques Kirouac.

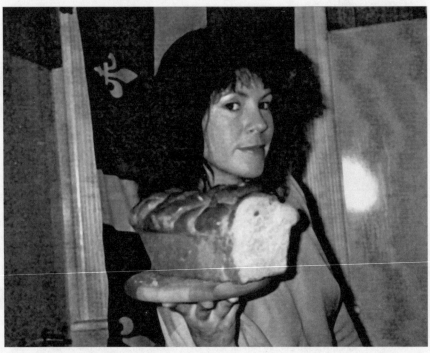

Jan with home-baked bread, and Quebec flag in background, Kingston, New York, 1989. Photo by Jacques Kirouac.

Jan rides to Grammies Awards ceremony with Allen Ginsberg in taxi, New York City, 1990. Photographer unknown.

Jan in Puerto Rico, just before her kidney failure, 1991. Photographer unknown.

Jan sits at her father's desk, 5169 – 10th Avenue North, St. Petersburg, Florida, March 1994. "That's the way the cookie crumbles, Jan." Photo courtesy of Jan Kerouac.

Jan at NYU Beat Generation conference, NYC, May 1994. Her second cousin, Paul Blake III, is on the left of her wearing New York Yankees hat. Photo by Lil Dodson.

Jan performs her rap song "Spice Cake" at NYU during Beat Generation conference, May 1994. Dave Amram on bongos at left. Photo by Gerald Nicosia.

Jan announces her lawsuit against the Sampas family, Gramercy Park Hotel, New York City, May 17, 1994. From left: Gerald Nicosia, Paul Blake III, Jan Kerouac, and Jan's attorney Thomas Brill. Photo by Sylvia Nicosia.

Jan at NYU Beat Generation Conference, New York City, May 1994, with her second cousin Paul Blake III behind her, and her father's friends, poet Ted Joans (at left) holding a "Kerouac Wears Khakis" poster, and journalist Al Aronowitz (at right). Photo by Gerald Nicosia.

Jan at Jack Kerouac's grave, Edson Cemetery, Lowell, Massachusetts, October 1994.
Photo by Chris Felver.

Brad Parker

REMEMBERING A LOST FRIEND

One of the Jack Kerouac biographies (*Jack Kerouac: King of the Beats* by Barry Miles) mentions me as the fellow who "arranged" for Jan Kerouac to appear in Lowell in 1988 for the dedication of a granite memorial to her father. And that is what, above all else, I was during the entire period of my friendship with Jan—"The Great Arranger." I was the one Lowell person who made sure that Jan (and her friend, Gerry Nicosia) spoke at public presentations in downtown Lowell, even though the "official" Kerouacians of that city never invited either of them there. Thus, Jan was in Lowell in 1988 and 1994, and Nicosia was there on four occasions between '88 and '96. It always seemed to me that if anyone had a right to be part of the ceremony honoring Lowell's greatest writer, Jan Kerouac had that right. I wondered why anyone would exclude Jack's daughter? And I was determined, also, to have Gerry Nicosia in Lowell because I was certain that his biography of Jan's father was the best biography available.

These events always threw my anxiety disorder into high gear, and in '94 I was writing in my private journal about the emotional "churning" in my mind prior to the public presentation by me, Jan, and Gerry. I wrote too that sponsoring this Kerouac program was creating a "storm" in certain Lowell circles, that I was popping more medication into my system to deal with the stress, but that somehow I relished the challenge.

Jan was supposed to be "beautiful"—at least that is how we envisioned her before her arrival in June of '88, when I met her at the Lowell train station. But the truly attractive young woman one views in photos from the late '70s was noticeably less beautiful a decade later at the age of 36. A few years following, Jan would suffer from renal failure and start the dialysis regimen that was part of her daily life until her death. Her second visit to Lowell demanded more baggage—she needed boxes of dialysis paraphernalia in her hotel room. I remember a photo of Jan in '88 in Lowell that included myself and Father Armand "Spike" Morissette. Father Morissette, then seventy-eight, was a local institution and the man who is credited with advising the young Jack Kerouac to go to New York City if he wished to become a writer. Almost fifty years later, he was supportive again, this time to Jack's daughter, providing a hotel room for Jan in '88. Father Spike lived to witness the courage of the father, Jack, who laid his life out in print for the world to see; plus, he saw the courage of the daughter who also risked public exposure and who came to Lowell in spite of local power-players who did not wish her there, at a time when "time" was a much more precious commodity for Jan than it had ever been.

As I write today, I can see Jan and her father staring at me from the back wall of my bedroom closet. The poster of Jan shows her standing at Jack's grave in the fall of '94, smiling and with her arms extended in a kind of "what now?" gesture. If I added a caption, it might be "Yup, *c'est moi* and my dad -- the 'naughty bummish fellow,' as I called him in *Baby Driver*, the guy who started this whole thing." Jan would later want to move her dad's remains to New Hampshire, where they could rest next to his beloved brother and his parents. It may, in fact, have been the choice Jack would have made (it certainly was his widow's choice in October of '69) but the "powers that be" in Lowell wouldn't let it happen. They always wanted to own the father, and were always indifferent to the daughter. Below the photo of Jan, filling up most of this black-and-white poster, is the poem she wrote about her still-born child—Natasha—born prematurely in Mexico in 1968, when Jan was not quite sixteen. It is a stark, sad bit of verse that seems detached from the pain that must have been part of Jan's internal landscape. She often buried pain, probably because there was so much of it in her life.

There are beer cans on Jack's grave in the poster, making me think of the self-destructive pattern that was his adult life, alongside the wealth of creativity with which he fashioned his books. And Jan's life had the same pattern of tragic self-destruction. I remember the remark she made in 1978 to Nicosia that her destiny was to be "pulverized." But the saving grace of her own creative abilities, fashioned from her own difficult existence, raised her up and apart from the moniker "Kerouac's daughter." She was, if you have not yet noticed, a good writer too. Maybe the caption to her photo should actually read: "Here we are, two writers, father and daughter—take your choice."

Jan participated in '88 in a forum on her father's "Lowell books." This particular event was sponsored by The Lowell Corporation for the Humanities, which I had set up a few years ealier. Initially, in '88, when I learned that there was an "official" Kerouac Committee planning to honor Jan's dad, I was quick to tell them—simply as a courtesy— that my non-profit corporation had already completed plans for bringing Gerry Nicosia to town, to speak alone, about the famous Kerouac. Later, I was stunned when one of the leaders of that committee tried verbal intimidation by telling me, via phone, that my plan had to change and that I should cooperate with him and his committee or I would become "a voice crying in the wilderness." Further, I was informed that they might find it necessary to "play hardball" with me, and that the hall I had reserved for Nicosia could be taken away from my organization. To say that I was angry is gross understatement, and I was positive that the "wilderness" would definitely be preferable to the city and the company of these power-brokers. I was certain then (and now) that someone was trying to please John Sampas, a major player on that committee, at the expense of ethics—but I eventually compromised and went ahead to organize the forum that included Jan, Nicosia, Regina Weinrich, John Tytell, Ann Charters, and Robin Moore.

Held in the evening at the Merrimack Repertory Theatre, the event was a success and raised about $300 for the homeless of Lowell, although Jan had some trouble reading her father's words. I didn't realize then that she had a vision problem and wondered why she stumbled with her dad's prose. She had told me that her favorite of her father's books (of those she had read) was *Lonesome Traveler*, but our program on June 23, 1988, did not include that work. Yet anyone reading Jack Kerouac's introduction to that book might find both father and daughter in his description of himself—a person of independent mind, familiar with city streets and drugs, an adventurer, a widely-traveled person who remained close to mother, and a person whose "special interests" included the opposite sex. But major differences are apparent too: he was well-educated, had a happier childhood, and became dedicated to writing while still in his teens. And if we delete the word "educated," we can use Jack's general characterization of *Lonesome Traveler* to cover the writings of both Kerouacs—"a mishmosh of life as lived by an independent . . . penniless rake going anywhere." Actually, I consider Jan to have been the more intrepid traveler of the two; she started doing the road thing earlier in life and, in my opinion, was a daughter who took on more risk than the father.

Six years later, in September, 1994, I arranged another public presentation that saw Jan and Gerry Nicosia speaking together at Middlesex Community College (situated very near to where her father worked for a Lowell newspaper in 1942), but she was feeling poorly that day. Her plane had been delayed in landing by a thunderstorm, and so she had been prevented from following her regular dialysis schedule. Nevertheless, she performed gamely. A celebration followed afterwards in Edson Hall behind Saint Anne's Espiscopal Church. That "party" included a cake, book and broadside signings by Gerry and Jan—who was described as appearing "wiped out" by Louise Hunt, one of the great women of Saint Anne's who oversaw the whole operation that night—and a visit by Allen Ginsberg, Jan's godfather and one of the men responsible for initiating a memorial to her father. Jan's lawsuit to recover her father's estate from the Sampas family had been filed earlier that year, and a Florida court had recently ruled in favor of allowing her case to proceed; hence the specially ordered cake. I do not recall that any of the "official" Lowell Kerouacians showed up for that party, although it's very likely that someone present at that celebration was a designated informant. Jan's and Gerry's Lowell opposition, always territorial (and sometimes paranoid), never seemed to lose an opportunity to monitor our public affairs. But the more opposition I sensed in my own native city, the more determined I became to continue my Kerouac presentations.

In her last taped interview, Jan said that the only possession of her father's that she owned was his DNA. Those who controlled Jack's estate had given her nothing that had been his. Her statement on that tape, which I still occasionally listen to, is the saddest remark I ever heard Jan utter.

Jan Kerouac: A Life in Memory

I am glad that my friendship with Jan came when it did, rather than when she was a teenager—the "saucy, unmanageable tart" she candidly describes in her first book. That relationship—with me still half-Puritan—would never have lifted off the ground. It was in her last years that, in my opinion, Jan Kerouac was doing a Princess Diana thing. This is to say, she was maturing, growing more secure within, and becoming more solidly her own person. The silly coquette routine had, I believe, been largely shed. And Jan was on a mission to save her deadbeat dad's literary legacy—manuscripts, letters, notebooks, etc.—from being dispersed to the far corners of the world (as she might say). Being gay, the strongest feelings I had for Jan were those of a brother and supportive friend. We would talk occasionally over those eight years via phone, sometimes about her upcoming visits to Lowell, and at other times about our mutual friend, Nicosia, or her belief that she would prevail in her lawsuit, or her writing, or my book about her dad, or her connection with Puerto Rico, an island familiar to both of us.

But, without a shade of doubt, the conversation that sticks more than any other in my mind is the one Jan and I had at the end of her first public visit to Lowell in 1988. We were together in my car, headed south from Lowell to a train station where I would say *hasta luego* to my new friend, while wondering if we would meet again. Along that route, I was overcome with a genuine, deep sadness for all the "tough stuff" that had been constantly threaded though Jan's life, and so I suggested that she settle down with a husband and child and live a more quiet, domestic life. Well, that got Jan fired up, and she rattled off the litany of her failed relationships with men, the loss of her baby in 1968, and the abortions and failed marriages that had followed. How could I possibly suggest that she could ever achieve what had always escaped her! She was telling me that she had done her best to find the happy life and she had failed; she was saying that such was not to be her lot—and how could I not realize that?! Her tirade, born of years of frustration and emotional pain, reminded me of Judy Garland's remark about never being able, in other than song, to find the other side of the rainbow. I knew that Jan's outburst was not any real anger at my question, but rather a deep exasperation at her own unsuccessful attempts to create a more stable, more satisfying, more truly joyful life. And I was silenced for the last few miles of our journey. I knew the foolishness of my question, yet I felt an even stronger empathy, and I knew that the despair she was expressing was horribly genuine. Then at the station, when she had her ticket in hand, I exercised my need to hug her and wish her well, and left her there to wait for the train that would take her, and other beaten travelers, on to whatever new destinations and experiences were awaiting them.

Today, when I think of Jan Kerouac, I think of a lost friend, and someone who needed more time but was denied it. I think of the girl who had been denied by her father, and who had later been denied any possession of his. I think too of the vulnerable, damaged woman who had learned early in life how to act to get attention, even if it was of a negative sort. I think of the harshness of her years of truancy and the lock-ups she was placed in as a juvenile, in New York City, the same urban setting where her father's life was forever changed in the decade prior to Jan's birth. I think of how Jack had tried to understand what had happened to him when, in his twenties, he was writing *The Town and the City*. It was a way to piece things together, to explain things about himself and his family and the world, just as Jan would later piece herself together in her several books to see more clearly who she was and where her niche in this world was; where she fit into the greater scheme of things.

She struggled with the identity stamped on her at birth—Kerouac's daughter—and she struggled with understanding that role; at the same time she was trying to pull together her own personal, unique role as a separate human being with an identity fully her own responsibility, and fully apart from anyone else in this universe. It was hard, very hard, and maybe she hadn't quite got the job done, maybe the obstacles were too great, but which one of us can say that we are finished products, that we have made it to the top of the mountain and do not need to climb any more? We all, in truth, fail when we are damaged and we never subsequently receive that vast quantity of love needed for the healing. That was true of Jack Kerouac, and it was true also of Janet Michelle Kerouac, whose rest now is well-deserved.

Dear Jan:

If you were here now, I would want to tell you that we did you proud in 1996 in Lowell. You were on the front of my t-shirt, facing that audience, and your dad was there too, on a t-shirt you had given me, the one with a portion of his final letter (October 20, 1969) reproduced on the reverse. It was the letter in which Jack stated that he did not wish his wife's Greek relatives in Lowell to inherit his estate. Remember—you mirrored that same sentiment in your last will and testament. Jim Jones, whom you did not want as your biographer, considers that part of your will to be "vicious," but I believe it came out of justifiable anger and your belief that your father's estate was obtained fraudulently, a question that no court has yet answered.

Jan, for that '96 Lowell memorial presentation, I read a portion of *Trainsong*—the section of that book that I find most affecting and emotionally wrenching. It was 1982 and you were in the house in Boulder where Peter Orlovsky and Allen Ginsberg were living—and you were experimenting with the word *daddy*. You were, as you tell us, a thirty-year-old woman saying that word "for the first time in her life"—whispering the word, "toying" with the syllables, screaming "DADDY." And you yell the word "louder and louder" so that your dad will be able to hear it, even in the "graveyard earth" of Edson Cemetery in Lowell, Massachusetts. Then, amazingly, your "primal cry" has summoned the essence of your father, and he is with you in that moment. You collapse onto the heater grate and have a talk with Jack; you even listen to his heart beat and peer into his "sad blue eyes." This was the man you had always looked for, sought out "over and over again" in your quest for love.

The former President of the Kerouac Family Association of Canada was there too, Jan. Jacques Kirouac delivered his heartfelt tribute to you, and several people, apart from myself, read from your books. One, David Daniel, is also a writer and had, at that time, five novels to his credit. Another reader was Helene Desjarlais of the Merrimack Repertory Theatre; she read your description of working on the movie *Heartbeat* about your dad's relationship with Neal and Carolyn Cassady. In addition, dear friend, we played a video of you—two interviews spliced together, 1995 and 1996. We wanted the audience to see you again, to hear your voice again. You told of the only two meetings you had with Jack, 1961 and 1967, and of your desire to have all of your father's archives safely in one place for scholars to access. Maybe you would even establish a "Kerouac House" along the model of Hemingway's preserved house in Key West, Florida. And you wanted to be remembered as the daughter who saved her dad's archives from "total destruction." You spoke against greed, and you spoke for posterity, and you spoke for your father's "honor." And, of course, your friend Gerry Nicosia spoke movingly and eloquently of your life and your spirituality, of the damage from your dad's absence, and of your wit, intelligence, and verbal skills. The finale, Jan, was a stunning rendition of "Amazing Grace" by Elyse O'Connor.

You know, dear Jan, if your father returned in human form long enough to write one more book, I would insist that he show the good grace to produce a work about you, and make his daughter into a legend, just as he had done with his pal, Neal Cassady. If a writer can take a sexually obsessed, irresponsible, highly neurotic, fast talking, clever con artist and make of him a saintly, heroic figure, then that same writer can damn well do something similar for his own kin. He could create another nonlinear "metaphysical study" using brilliant parodies, and you—in addition to Cassady—would be a representative of America. He could again blow away objective reality in a continuing exploration of love and friendship; he could again use his sharp wit, his storehouse of knowledge, and his light-hearted touch to redeem the life of his own flesh from darkness. So finally, with such a tome completed, your dad would have fully embraced and recognized you, and would have combined all his great literary skills to create a work that we might today call *Visions of Lost Michelle*. Then, future readers would have a book that ends in a fashion similar to *Visions of Cody,* just changed for the gender: not good-bye to any "king" on the final page—rather, "Adios, Queen."

Aram Saroyan

CHILDREN OF THE FAMOUS: THE FINAL EVOLUTION OF JAN KEROUAC

One lunch hour during the spring of 1995 I drove up to the Ventura Bookstore to have Allen Ginsberg sign a copy of his new book, *Cosmopolitan Greetings*. The line was a long one, with many more people behind me; but when I got to Allen I'd decided that I'd try to say something on behalf of Jan Kerouac. There was to be a conference on Jack Kerouac's writings at New York University that June, and Jack Kerouac's only child, Jan, a novelist in the stylistic tradition of the Beats, had been excluded. At the same time, Jan was challenging the right of the family of her father's last wife, Stella Sampas, to control the Kerouac estate. She believed the will of her grandmother and Kerouac's mother, Gabrielle, which turned everything over to Stella, had been forged.

Since Stella's death, control of the estate had passed to her brother John Sampas. Jan wanted her father's papers in one place, a special collections library, and word was that both the New York Public Library and the Bancroft Library of the University of California at Berkeley had offered $1,000,000 for the archive, but that John Sampas hadn't accepted either offer and was selling off items piecemeal. He had sold Kerouac's raincoat and at least a couple of Kerouac letters to Johnny

Depp for over $20,000. If he sold the estate piece by piece it was clear that he could make many times the amount offered for the archive en masse, Kerouac's vogue being at its height.

The biographer Barry Miles explained to me that the reason a Kerouac first edition goes today for as much as or more than one by Charles Dickens, for instance, is that the people who read Kerouac in their youth are now in their fifties and at the peak of their careers. These are the readers for whom Kerouac historically will have meant the most, hence his price has peaked and can be expected in time to level out.

As the son of another writer, William Saroyan, whose estate had been the subject of dispute and bad feelings, I wanted to put in a word on behalf of the writer's immediate family. I had never met Jan, but in recent months had spoken with her on the phone regarding legal help with her claim to the estate, and my sympathies were with her. Strikingly attractive as a young woman while looking very much the Kerouac, she had traveled a hard road in life, and now in her early forties was on dialysis for kidney failure. She sounded on the phone like a sweet lost soul who, late in the day, was trying to assume a place that in a more equitable world would have been hers from the outset. In fact she had seen her father only twice, although after a blood test Kerouac had finally acknowledged that she was his daughter.

Allen and I greeted each other. I handed him my open book to be signed and said something about feeling bad about what was happening with Jan Kerouac, having had similar troubles in my own family.

I recognized the importance of Jan's effort on two different levels. On the one hand, she was behaving as a dutiful daughter, herself an established novelist, in attempting to keep her father's archives and other belongings intact and to make them readily available to the scholarly community. At the same time, she was belatedly assuming the role of a mature adult in taking her place as her father's most legitimate heir. It was this part of her effort that seemed to me to be the more difficult for her. It was also quite evidently life-sustaining to her.

The children of the famous are often shunted aside in the posthumous sweepstakes that can occur among those who establish various claims on the deceased, and it isn't uncommon for these children to assume a fatalistically accepting stance as their own interests are dismissed. I recognized that Jan, in an advanced stage of her disease, was struggling mightily against any such tendency in herself. Allen looked up from his book at me and for a moment seemed to be puzzling something out in my face.

"I smell Nicosia somewhere behind this," he said.

He was referring to my friend, Kerouac's biographer Gerald Nicosia, and while it was true I'd originally heard of Jan's troubles from Gerry, he hadn't had to coax my sympathy. Nicosia had in the meantime been organizing a fund raiser to help Jan with her medical bills and told me Allen had called friends like Gary Snyder and Michael McClure and discouraged their participation. I acknowledged that I had heard about it from Gerry, but that...

"Look," Allen said with uncharacteristic vehemence, "I spent several days researching Nicosia's charges, did you do that?" I acknowledged that I hadn't, and he went on to say that he had found them to be unsubstantiated.

What struck me most as Allen spoke was how frail he seemed. I'd seen him just a month earlier reading at UC Santa Barbara, and while he was wonderful, I'd noticed then that he'd aged since I'd seen him read there three years earlier. Now at the bookstore, having never seen him so agitated, I backed off and softened my tone, and tried to finish our exchange so that the line wouldn't be stalled any longer. While we'd been talking, Allen had continued to doodle on his title page and he gave me back an inscription with unusually elaborate decorations.

As the New York University conference drew near, I spoke with Gerry and Jan regarding doing their own press conference in Manhattan, which they did on the opening day of the event. With some of the participants having a claim to being there far less valid than Jan Kerouac's, she along with Gerry Nicosia was thrown out of the conference by campus police when she attempted to get on the podium and speak about her father's archives. Braving the hostility of many who would appropriate her father's legacy for their own purposes, Jan Kerouac grew in stature in her last year even as she succumbed physically. In addition to being the gifted novelist that she was, she emerged as a person of rare courage.

I called Gerry in Northern California when I heard that Jan had died. Her white blood cell count had gone precipitously down, he told me, and she'd gone into a hospital in Albuquerque, where she lived again after a brief time in Marin County. They had removed her spleen, but she had survived only a few hours after the operation. Jan had been ill for some time and the news wasn't wholly unexpected, but I'm still confounded by the lack of sympathy shown to this benighted woman by Allen Ginsberg and others. Gerry said she had died a year to the day after she'd been thrown out of the conference.

Brenda Knight

THE AQUARIAN CONNECTION: JAN'S LAST PHONE CALLS

Beat poet ruth weiss orchestrated my connection with Jan Kerouac. On ruth's word that I was neither a flake nor a user, Jan agreed to talk. She greeted my call with obvious suspicion, sounding wary and rather weary as well. She could hardly believe that, for once, someone was calling about her mother, Joan, and not about her father, Jack. At the time, I was working on an anthology of the women Beats. Once she figured out this really wasn't a ruse, we got along like a house afire. We set up a series of interviews and, about halfway through, she generously offered to write an original essay recounting her memories of her mother for my book. I still have the manila envelope and the letters in her big rangy handwriting. Like me, she used a many-times resent manila envelope, and I smiled to have found a fellow planet-lover.

Jan was sick at the time and getting sicker. She had to have kidney dialysis four times a day, and I had a toll-free number at work, so Jan got in habit of calling me during dialysis. She said "talking to you makes the time go faster." We ended up having a great deal in common—we were both deeply interested in astrology, reincarnation, tarot, and all manner of metaphysics. She wove this fascination with the mystical into her work, too. *Parrot Fever* pulses with it. She surmised our immediate friendship "was the Aquarian vibration"; she was born

105

February 16th and I was born February 19th, which actually put me on the cusp of Pisces and Aquarius.

It was enjoyable to talk to someone as knowledgeable as Jan on these subjects; she was curious and caring and spoke with an easy grace and wisdom born of experience. According to her, it was the hard-won wisdom of many lifetimes. Jan was special, even astrologically — a Water Dragon in the Chinese zodiac, dragons being the most auspicious of all signs, the most powerful, the most dynamic and the most charismatic. In Jan's case, it served to make her beautiful, inside and out. I, on the other hand, was her exact opposite in Chinese astrology. "Jan, I'm a double Pisces Dog, just like your Dad," I said. I still remember the laughter, a kind of crackling purr coming over the phone line.

I came to look forward to the daily calls on my toll-free number. We had wide-ranging conversations. She shared tales from her wild childhood; she spoke of her hopes for her work-in-progress, *Parrot Fever*. Jan talked a lot about her mother, Joan Haverty Kerouac, and how they moved around from San Francisco to Oregon and Washington State. Her mother was a most unusual woman who had an idiosyncratic gardening style, a habit of dismantling walls, and an inability to feel physical pain. Jan was deeply moved when her mother decided to write her own autobiography after being diagnosed with breast cancer and given mere months to live. Jan's memories were clear, her love for her mother shining through:

"I remember watching mom, her bony frame in her favorite antique turquoise sweatshirt, shuffling over to sit down at her typewriter. It was an ancient machine, covered with tobacco dust. She would sit down every evening, or whenever she got a chance, and between intermittent gulps of coffee, and drags on her hand-rolled Bugler-tobacco cigarettes, she would tap away with one finger on each hand. She was my greatest friend and confidante."

Against all conventional wisdom, Jan's mother lived eight years longer than the prognosis and produced thousands of pages of her memoir. Jan recounted the family's amazement as they kept finding more manuscript pages hidden under the bed and stuffed in the walls after Joan's death. I wondered if Jan was repeating her mother's death-defying writing project with *Parrot Fever*.

Jan got a kick out of the fact that I was moving from the Haight district in San Francisco to a tiny alley in Russian Hill. Through some bizarre coincidence, the first place I looked at, and fell in love with, was a cottage directly across from 29 Russell Street, where Jack Kerouac had stayed with Neal and Carolyn Cassady. She was insistent it was "karma" and proof of my past life connection to the Beats and, more importantly, to her. I told her I could stand on my bedroom balcony and look into the window of the upstairs room where Jack slept and worked on *Visions of Cody* and wrote many a letter. We made plans for her to come stay with me and take a series of photos of us like the famous one now gracing the cover of *On the Road*, of Neal and Jack hugging in front of a window, a window that I now look out of from my office.

Jan and her dad's paths only crossed twice in life, but they also talked on the phone, Jack Kerouac waxing sentimental about the idea that she would follow in his footsteps and be a writer, too. He revealed their royal ancestry, "You're not a Canuck, you're a Bretonne," intimating his belief that she was indeed his daughter in every way. Some of the most lively conversations of all were Jan's recollections of her time on the road and on the rails, "from Camden to Casablanca," on freighters and freight trains, working myriad odd jobs — baker, groom, stripper, fisherman, actress in the movie *Heartbeat*, maid, and, of course, writer.

Jan also shared her fears with me about the fate of her father's literary legacy. She spoke of the fight she and her champion, Gerry Nicosia, waged with Jack Kerouac's widow's family, the Sampases. She loved telling the story about how she and Gerry disrupted a Beat hagiography at NYU, shouting and protesting the appropriation of Jack Kerouac's estate, from his writing right down to an old overcoat that was eventually sold to actor Johnny Depp: "I just want his work to stay all in one place and not be sold off piece by piece." Jan seemed pleased she and Gerry created lots of controversy and got kicked out. However, Jan was hurt by what she deemed the cowardice of most of the "players" in the Beat scene. She said she felt the most support from William Burroughs and Gregory Corso, interestingly enough. Burroughs had provided one of his original artworks for a fundraiser for Jan, and Corso was one of the few Beats to sign a petition for her right to speak at the NYU conference. She noted they were the real "outlaws," and hadn't gone soft and bourgeois.

My main interest in Jan was her unique sensibility. The hoopla about her parentage was entirely secondary. Her father could have been an insurance salesman who wrote policies instead of epoch-making novels and Jan Kerouac would still have been a larger-than-life persona, so real as to be super-real. As a writer, Jan had a distinctive voice; I thought of her as a neopsychedelic writer, perhaps more akin to Ken Kesey than Jack Kerouac. She told me she aspired to "magical realism" in her writing.

Her prose is awash with layers of meaning and a matchless rhythm and flow. Jan's writing sparkles, really, much in the way as Jan did as a person, which my fellow Beat scholar and researcher, the late Jay Kahn, and I discovered when we drove down to Albuquerque to visit her. I couldn't help but marvel how her process differed so from her dad's avowedly tortured labors. Jack Kerouac, undeniably brilliant, hoed and chiseled away at his writing like a field hand; this we know from his many letters telling us so.

"I know I have my own style of writing, which is very different from Jack's," Jan said. "People may read my stuff and think, 'This is Jack Kerouac's daughter, let's see if she's as good as he is.' But, it's not necessary to make a comparison like that because I wasn't trying to emulate his type of writing."

With Jan, you got the feeling that words spun out of her like a gossamer web. She loved words and it shows. Moreover, Jan wrote like she spoke, an invaluable asset as her eyes started to fail and she was forced to begin recording *Parrot Fever* onto tapes. I asked her why she was experiencing such severe vision problems and she replied simply, "Too much acid. I used to drop liquid acid directly onto my eyeballs. That way, it goes directly into your bloodstream and hits your brain faster; the hallucinations are incredible. You should try it at least once." For all my would-be hipness, I sat on the other end of the line feeling like a young Republican. I realized Jan Kerouac had compressed many lifetimes in this one. Time wasn't on her side, but she was a living filament, lit from within.

In fact, Jan Kerouac was dying, but she was more alive than anyone else I knew. Through my book *Women of the Beat Generation* and this one, the result of the dedication of Gerry Nicosia and Phil Cousineau, Jan Kerouac lives on. When *Women of the Beat Generation* was published, the poets and I did a series of unforgettable readings we came to refer to as "gynocentric poetry slams," and I read around the country with the grand ladies from this singular genre. We were brokenhearted that Jan had died in June, 1996, as she had been so excited about the literary tour, the chance to see so many of the women she knew like Carolyn Cassady, Diane di Prima, Eileen Kaufman, and Hettie Jones, to name but a few, and also the men like Ted Joans and Michael Mc-Clure.

Even after her death, though, Jan made her presence known. I would notice people flipping through the anthology, always stopping when they got to Jan's chapter. Nobody could move past the incandescent photos of Jan. Two are particularly striking. In the first, a young Jan Kerouac looks away from the camera; some idea has caught her fancy, and her fierce intelligence combined with an even fiercer beauty draws the eye and won't let go. The other photo is Jan, atop the Hollywood Hills, full-face to the camera. Her essence, a joyous free sprit open-armed to life, is captured here. Young men are especially mesmerized, gazing upon the photos of Jan, invariably speaking of her in the present tense, "Where is she? Let's go find her!"

I always wordlessly wish them well on their journey to find her. I feel like I know where they might happen upon Jan Kerouac—she's on the road, her *own* road.

Lynn Kushel Archer

JAN KEROUAC: MY BOSS AND FRIEND

Jan's last dream was to see *Parrot Fever* published. Jan and I raced from April 1994 until her death in June of 1996 to finalize *Parrot Fever*. I transcribed her tapes and transferred her handwritten pages into the computer. Her tale is pure poetry, captivating and riveting, with a talent not unlike her renowned father's. We built up a close and loving friendship as she told me of her extraordinary, unusual life.

I knew Jan during the last few years of her life. The first months we worked together we corresponded by phone and mail while she was living in Albuquerque. Jan and I both grew up in New York. I retained the accent. She, on the other hand, had an elegant and cheery voice, but if she needed to, she could sound like a 300-pound teamster. We found comfort in our shared New Yorkiness. When she moved to Marin in the summer of 1995, we became closer.

At one point that summer, she had a wound on her foot that was originally diagnosed as a brown recluse spider bite, but this wound was finally diagnosed as related to her kidney problems. For months it hurt her when she walked, but she insisted on wearing high heels anyway. She would always "dress" for an occasion—even if it was just to go to the doctor or the store to pick up a Marie Callender favorite. Jan was beautiful: slim, crystal ball-like eyes, large lovely lips, and a voice that was gentle and soft, sort of crackly, like a little old lady's.

She loved comedy. She used highfalutin words for the most mundane activities and giggled on the tapes as she would share comedy segments on TV with me. She once described a Woody Allen segment in detail. She was wonderful and fun to be with. One tape she started off: "Hello testes, ya got one . . . two." The last words on her last tape were her Porky Pig impression: "Th-th-th-that's all, folks!" She made me laugh a lot.

It was difficult for her to both write and read because of her failing motor skills. I printed her manuscripts in extra large type. She was doing abdominal dialysis, "exchanges" as she would call them, four times a day. These handicaps frustrated her, but she was never bitter, whiny or morose. She had too many dreams to fulfill. I'll enumerate them:

First, she was determined to finish *Parrot Fever*.

Second, she wanted to get started on her autobiography.

Third, she wanted to write her next novel.

Fourth, she wanted to open up Kerouac's, a San Francisco restaurant. I wish I'd known her in her cooking days. She prided herself on her cooking abilities. She savored each morsel of life. She was a true artist—editing, intensifying and clarifying her dynamic life for us all. She had so much good to share.

Fifth, she wanted her father's archives to be available to all. She loved and admired her father. Why wouldn't she follow in his footsteps? Her memory was astoundingly acute like his. She would say, "I'm a genius like my Dad." She certainly was.

She had many goals that she was working towards, and lots of obstacles.

While she never missed her dialysis, she was casual about the circumstances of her "exchanges," and often performed them in front of close friends. She would always manage to find a bed to lie down on no matter where she was. She moved four times in the short time I knew her. She traveled often across the country fighting to right her father's estate. What fortitude and perseverance for someone so ill. She did not despair. She was on the road and determined to get her dreams realized.

Many of the tapes she sent me were sort of like "hanging out together" while she collected her thoughts for the book. They were easy and entertaining to transcribe. She would do each one in just one take. I'd never have to roll back the tape. It was amazing how fast and perfectly woven her words would be. As she told me the story of her life, editing it for fiction, I was always surprised by her perceptive words. Poetic pearl after pearl, without any hesitation, would gently fall from her lips. Her words were delicate drops of textual images as she remembered the tiniest of details. It was thrilling to transcribe her thought. Right now I really admire that talent as I'm struggling to write this short piece in her honor. I haven't written anything but lists in the last 20 years. This is not easy. What talent and brilliance she had.

At times she would warm up trying to get her thoughts in order for the book, and she'd fill a whole side of tape singing. She could sing. I mean she could really sing! Her impressions were impeccable. She would do impressions of Smoky Robinson, Carol King, Hindi motion picture songs she had memorized, Aretha, The Doors, Billie Holiday, The Four Tops, and Patsy Cline. She was amazing.

She did not take guff from anybody. She was fiercely independent, like her Mom who raised her alone. It was hard for her to maintain her independence with her illness, but she did. She would hobble to downtown San Anselmo to sit in a coffee shop and eat something delectable as she observed everybody and everything.

When she moved to Marin I tried to help her as much as I could. She did not drive. I would take her to the doctors and stores. We chatted on the phone, or she hung out at my place. I helped her with her moves. We would go to the dump loaded with her empty Baxter "exchange" boxes (which would accumulate into a truck load in a few weeks). I was lucky, she was always appreciative and not demanding towards me.

She had discerning tastes and was very demanding of herself and others. When we went out to eat I began to expect a little bit of a scene with the wait-staff because of those discerning tastes.

An excerpt from one of her tapes follows:

"I wonder if anyone will ever listen to this tape later besides you. Oh well, someday when, ya know, when they're doing archeology and digging up garbage from the 20th century, this will be in the garbage somewhere and they'll put in the tape and it'll sound all horrible and *uch*. I just baked one of those Marie Callender cherry pies and I'm trying to carry it to the table with my bare fingers and burned myself a little bit. And now I'm going to endeavor to eat it. It's pretty good. You should try 'em. I don't know if you've tried these. Anything Marie Callender does is really good. You can't even really tell it's a frozen thing. That's what I think. And I've got pretty damn discerning tastes. I suppose I should turn off the tape while I'm eating [mouth full]. I don't feel like it."

Jan was only self-deprecating when she talked of her relationships with men. She described one guy ("such a braggart and swashbuckler") she picked up in a bar in Oregon: "He was more interested in telling all the guys at the bar evidently than he was in even hanging around with me which was usually the case. 'Cause all the guys I would pick would be guys who would ignore me or abuse me verbally or something because of this father complex I have."

She had a tremendous responsibility to carry on Jack Kerouac's legacy. Her novels and poems are brilliant in the same tradition as her Dad's writings. He had no one to look up to, but she certainly did. In the short time she was alive she wrote three exquisite novels. Her father definitely would have been proud.

As Jan's trying to figure out *Parrot Fever's* story line she says:

"... Maxine's reeling in the ropes and stuff and she almost passes out and falls overboard. Maybe I should have her really fall overboard and then that would be more of an adventure. In life things almost happen, but in fiction they could really happen."

It thrilled her to realize that potential. I wished she had lived long enough to have written the last few segments that would have tied up the loose ends of *Parrot Fever*. Jan had so much joy and articulate reflections to share. The world has been deprived because she died so

young. I was honored to have known this fabulously uplifting, productive, bright, creative and caring artist. I will love and miss her always.

Forest Knolls, California, June, 2002

Kerouac wore khakis.

"Kerouac Wore Khakis" (later changed to "Kerouac Wears Khakis") poster created by Jan Kerouac to protest sale of her father's image for a Gap ad by the Sampas family. Photo by Jack Newsom.

Jan Kerouac speaking about her lawsuit at press conference, the San Francisco Press Club, March 1995, photo by Greg Aston.

Below: Jan performs with her half-brother David Bowers at a benefit for her medical and legal expenses, Cowell Theater, Fort Mason, San Francisco, April 1, 1995. According to Dan McKenzie, Jack Kerouac's ghost waited just offstage. Photo by Greg Aston.

John Cassady and Jan at Enrico's Sidewalk Café, April 1, 1995. "Do you remember me asking you to marry me that day?" Photo by Danielle La Near.

Jan and ex-boxer Ira Carter outside the Roxie Theater, San Francisco, March 28, 1995: "He's the man who took my virginity." Photo by Eric Predoehl.

Jan and her cousin Paul Blake, Jr., at Nicosia home in Corte Madera, California, April 2, 1995. Photo by Gerald Nicosia.

Jan meets with librarian Tony Bliss at the Bancroft Library, University of California, Berkeley, to see about finding a permanent home for all of her father's papers and manuscripts. Photo by Gerald Nicosia.

Historic moment, June 5, 1995, as Jan and Jacques Kirouac are blocked from ascending the stage by NYU Programs Director Helen Kelly at Beat Generation conference. Anne Waldman looks on from the podium. Photo by Gerald Nicosia.

Jan and Jacques Kirouac in Washington Square Park, New York City, June 5, 1995, after being thrown out of NYU's Jack Kerouac conference. Jan wears t-shirt she had printed up with the text of her father's last letter (October 20, 1969) to Paul Blake, Jr., stating that he did not want the Sampas family to get any of his estate. Photo by Mary Emmerick.

Jan with Vietnam veteran Bobby Waddell on left and Jacques Kirouac on right hold up banner outside Town Hall in New York City during NYU Beat conference performance from which she had been excluded. Photo by Duarte Moniz.

Jan's shrine to both her parents, Albuquerque, fall 1995. Photo courtesy of Jan Kerouac.

Jan and Lee Harris in photomat booth, doing horror movie imitations, Los Angeles, March 1996. Photo courtesy of Lee Harris.

Jan, circa April 1996 (in one of her last known photographs, about two months before she died), demonstrates her determination to continue fighting the Sampas family to recover her inheritance and to preserve her father's literary archive. Photo courtesy of Jan Kerouac.

R.B. Morris

THE SPIRIT OF A KEROUAC

I met Jan Kerouac in 1982 in Boulder, Colorado. I was catching a ride across town with her and Gerry Nicosia, photographer Chris Felver, and a couple of other people in Gerry's car. Everyone was there for the *On The Road* conference. I had just spent about 3 days thumbing over from East Tennessee and was sleeping on the floor of the house where Gerry was staying. I was a ghost of a hobo chasing around the ghost of Jack Kerouac, and all of a sudden I'm riding in the backseat of a car with his daughter.

Gerry introduced us and told her I was from Tennessee. She said "Tennessee" a couple of times slowly, and told me she had always loved the sound of that word. She asked if that wasn't a Native American name, and noted how certain states have Native American names. We thought of others like Alabama, Minnesota, Mississippi, and talked about the sounds of the names. We had a very pleasant and funny conversation that ended far too soon.

Jan Kerouac was absolutely stunning, probably at the peak of her health and beauty then. Her big blue eyes were wildly mesmerizing, and I felt like everyone at the conference was falling in love with her. If not, they were at least captivated by her presence, which was like a young Jack Kerouac come back in the flesh of a girl. She was the unsuspected star of that show. At that time there was still some question as to whether she was actually Jack's daughter. Apparently, a lot of people just didn't want her to be. I think her presence at the conference, where she was a featured reader, went a long way toward dispelling doubts about her lineage. She was undeniably Kerouac.

I hadn't read her first book at the time, and didn't know but a small part of her story. I guess that's all we ever know, but later I did learn more of the many lives she led, a wild far-flung and unforgiving tale. It looked like she got a lot of bad breaks, and was surely cheated out of a few things too by people who shouldn't have turned on her or forgotten her. Then sickness and early death. A tough story and sad. But you know I never felt too badly for Jan Kerouac because she was always above it. She had such a strong and determined spirit. She could be robbed of a lot, but not that.

I was in New York in '94 at one of the NYU conferences the last time I saw her. It was a long ways from that first meeting in Boulder, and not too long before she died. She was on dialysis by then, and having a lot of physical problems. By that time, she was being ostracized by the Beat community and fighting a legal battle with the Sampases over the estate, very courageously taking her case to the people. I don't think a lot of the attendees at the conference knew the kind of physical pain she was experiencing, and how it affected her ability to focus when she was reading or speaking.

We were at the hotel where Nicosia was staying when we last spoke. She was telling me how she'd love to make a country music record, how she loved to sing. We caught an elevator down to the lobby and walked out on the street, going different ways. She gave me a hug, said, "It's good to see you again," and wished me luck. I said the same, and she was gone.

Buddah (John Paul Pirolli)

TWO CHILDREN OF THE SIXTIES

Jan Kerouac and I met over the phone thanks to our great mutual friend, Gerry Nicosia, and we quickly became fast friends. As our friendship grew, I started writing poetry about her. My poems about her got longer and longer. They eventually became a chronology of her struggles: telling the people at different poetry readings in the New England area about was happening in her battle to free her father's works.

Then we decided to write a book together using my poetry and her prose. The book was to be called *Daughter of Duluoz*. It was to be a continuation of her life story, telling the stories she missed in her first two semiautobiographical books, *Baby Driver* and *Trainsong*.

The idea for the book came from our lengthy weekly phone conversations. We realized we were both children of the Sixties, and had multiple mutual memories—like our mutual love of *Mad* magazine. For example, on our last tragic phone call, I sang to her from a parody of a Broadway Show, "Mad about the Sixties," a compilation of materials taken from *Mad* magazine from the Sixties. The song is called "Wouldn't It Be Kerouac?" sung to the tune of "Wouldn't It Be Loverly?" from *My Fair Lady*. Before I could finish the song, she was rushed away from the phone by her ex-sister-in-law, Deborah Bower. I never spoke to Jan again.

Jan and I would talk about our mutual memories, and this would trigger other memories Jan had about her childhood. An example of such a triggered conversation was the time we talked about one of Jan's favorite New York City staples, egg creams. Being raised in the Boston area, I had only heard about egg creams on New York-based television shows like *The Tonight Show* with Johnny Carson, before he moved the show to California. I remembered a specific show when Jerry Lewis actually brought egg creams on stage. Finally, while traveling through New York to college in Kentucky, I got to try one. *WOW!*

Jan and I started to talk about egg creams after we had talked about our mutual memory of Jerry Lewis's appearance. In those days, late in her life, Jan was living on cans of Ensure, smuggled to her for free by the nurses at Lovelace Hospital in Albuquerque. When I asked her what Ensure tasted like, she said, "Oh, it tastes just like egg creams." At one point, in fact, she told me her diet consisted of one or two cans of Ensure and a potato a day.

Let me back up for a second. In 1994, John Sampas, the executor of Stella Sampas Kerouac's estate, which contained all of Jack Kerouac's papers and copyrights, told Jan that he was planning to let a collection of her father's letters be published, as well as a collection of other Kerouac pieces called *The Portable Kerouac*. He was going to let Ann Charters do the editing. In Jan's eyes, this meant there would probably be censorship of her father's writing, and that anything pertaining to Jack's planned divorce from Stella (his last wife) or his bisexual experiences—among other things—would probably never see the light of day. Due to the fact Jan had already started litigation against John Sampas, he needed her permission to do those books. Jan did not want Ann Charters as editor, choosing our mutual friend Gerry Nicosia instead. Sampas told Jan through his sharkster lawyers that she either sign the contract or he would have her share of her father's foreign royalties stopped. Those royalties were an essential part of Jan's income. She was pressured to sign. Shortly thereafter Sampas had Jan's foreign royalties stopped anyways. The loss of those royalties put a serious dent in her income, which was already stretched thin with a raft of medical and legal expenses.

In the last few months of her life, Jan paid her rent with borrowed money and—in my opinion—literally starved to death. I remember how she, being a gourmet cook, would lovingly describe how she would cook that one potato. She would tell me about the herbs and spices she could use—how cooking it reminded her of her days as a pastry chef in Santa Fe, making a special peach desert for some famous movie starlet. But it was still one damn potato a day, no matter how she cooked it, while John Sampas sat on millions of dollars that—in my opinion—should have been hers.

Let me explain why I call Jan my sister. I am the head of an international fraternal and esoteric organization, named the Sacred and Mystical Order of the Sword and Shield. I am also one of the two cardinal/archbishops of the Independent Gnostic Catholic Charismatic Church in North America. Jan Michelle Kerouac was initiated as my sister in the Sword and Shield in May 1995, at the Gramercy Park Hotel in New York City. As our friendship grew, she became more than a fraternal sister. She became the baby sister I always wanted.

In her last months, Jan and I would have dozens of fantastically long telephone conversations. Because these conversations triggered such great memories, I suggested that we tape them, then edit out the stones and water, and add the poetry I had already written, to create a book. Jan loved the idea. Due to the little known fact that she was losing her eyesight, Jan had become proficient in using her tape recorder, to write what was going to be her third book, *Parrot Fever*. *Daughter of Duluoz* would have been her fourth book and my second. We were supposed to start the book in the summer of 1996, but for Jan, that summer never came.

The title of this book came from another rambling conversation I had with Jan. I was reading to Jan the first page of text from her dad's book *Big Sur*. Jack was telling how he planned to put his stories into chronological order and call them *The Duluoz Legend*. He wrote that because of the objections of earlier publishers, he was not allowed to use the same personae names in each of his books, but that in his old age he would collect them all in one large work called *The Duluoz Legend*, reinserting a complete set of uniform names. Then, he wrote, he could die happy. Of course, Jack didn't have a chance for an old age or to die happy, any more than Jan did.

After I read this passage to Jan, we decided that since Jack was calling himself Duluoz, then Jan would be "The Daughter of Duluoz." Thus came the title of our book.

On June 5th, 1996, Jan died. That was less than a week from the time I sang to her. Later that summer, I decided to continue the work we had planned to collaborate on. My book is dedicated to her memory. It is also dedicated "to Gerald Nicosia, the battling Scorpio from Corte Madera, and to my son, Jan's namesake, John Michael Pirolli."

[EDITOR'S NOTE: Buddah simplifies the many years of legal battles Jan Kerouac had with John Sampas and his family, but his brief version is essentially true. After three years (1982-1985) of wrangling with the Sampases, Jan was finally accorded the fifty percent share of her father's royalties that U.S. Copyright Law said was due to her. However, that law only specified that Jan was owed half of her dad's U.S. royalties. The Sampases, either from generosity or misunderstanding the law, also began paying her half of some of Jack Kerouac's foreign royalties as well. Once she sued their family in 1994, and they discovered their error, they threatened to withhold those foreign royalties unless she went along with their plans to publish new Kerouac titles, which included — against Jan's wishes — using Ann Charters as an editor. Jan went along with John Sampas in order to keep those foreign royalties, and then, as Buddah states, John Sampas turned around and shut off her share of her dad's foreign royalties anyway. The Sampases argued that they were acting within the law by doing so. But there was certainly an alternative legal opinion, which was that since Jan had been paid those royalties for several years, she had grown dependent on them and was still entitled to them. That legal doctrine is called *laches*, which in essence means that if you don't do something (such as withholding royalties) when you're supposed to, you are barred from doing it later on. The argument over those withheld foreign royalties was still going on when Jan died. All of these facts can be verified in Jan Kerouac's archive, which includes all of her voluminous legal papers, on deposit at the University of California's Bancroft Library.]

Dan McKenzie

THE GREAT, SAD, INDIAN HEART OF JAN KEROUAC

Gazing upon a winsome goddess trying to give what they wanted, I saw, to quote Jim Morrison, "the warm connectors" slowly draining what personal power she had left to enliven their dull, jealous, mundane heresies of token alignments in their endless thirst to fill their unfillable, vacant, empty, insensitivities, in that absurd notion that they are immortal and can afford to be careless. Careless with a beautifully naive and aching sylph, yet even more careless with their personal atrocities against themselves and this ethereal being because they feel they will not have to account for their actions nor have any hope of redemption and in the name of amassment, recognition, and perhaps the Tantalusian concept called fame, exploit an already self-condemned, haunted, sweet entity of prose and creativity trying to live up to the wastrel image of her father, ole Pisces Jack, an artist of superb prose and especially feeling but with an undoing trap-door of self-indulgence that eventually killed him. I considered the Kerouac sublime gift and lesson as I watched her walk.

At long last she bridged to me, and quickly I learned that she was more at home speaking Mexican as she had been living in New Mexico and had loved that cold, death-like, chaparral desert as do I.

"I couldn't help but notice that you are not well," I said quietly

133

to her in *la lengua bonita*. With a sweet, sad light within her eyes she slowly answered, "*Si, es la verdad. No me siento bien … parece no tengo la fuerza para vivir. Quisiera llorar todo el tiempo…*" [Yes, it's true. I don't feel well … like I don't have the energy to live. I feel like crying all the time.]

Seeing into her great, sad heart that wanted to cry all the time as she had just whispered to me in Mexican, I followed her feeling looking for an answer when I suddenly stated, "*Las medicinas de los Indios son más mejor porque tienen espíritu natural. Quidado con los Doctores Americanos y las medicinas ellos traígan. No te dejes, trucha con los que no son gente, me simpatizo, Jan Kerouac.*" ["The medicines of the Indians are much stronger because they have natural spirit. Be careful with the American doctors and the medicines they bring. Don't let yourself … watch out for those who aren't the people — my sympathies, Jan Kerouac."]

Within a seemingly endless moment whilst she searched my feeling for truth, I switched languages.

"Jan, you have been drained and drained of your finite personal power by '*Ellos que no son gente,*' 'those who are not human,' and it takes energy to maintain one's equilibrium and one's continuity as we move about and avoid the 'phantoms.' *Medicinas herbales de los Indios tienen fuerza y espíritu perfectamente para nosotros. Pero, necesitamos fuerza personal … tanto … tanto necesitamos. Y los corazones oscuros que no tienen alma o vida quieren usar su fuerza solamente, ya mero nos moriremos. Ellos no les gustan usted … no les gustan tú, Jan Kerouac. No te dejas, trucha con ellos que no tienen luz.*" ["Herbal medicines of the Indians have strength and spirit that are perfect for us. But we need personal strength … need it so … so much. And the dark hearts that have no soul or life want to use your strength, they almost kill us. They don't like you, Jan Kerouac. Don't let yourself … stay alert against those who have no light."]

That beautiful sylph barely able to stay here upon our beloved Mother that energizes all, skin already like leather, smiled upon me and with tears issuing forth from her marvelous, living eyes, slowly said quietly, "I know they don't give a fig for me nor like or love me. But I just don't feel I have enough strength to ward off their injurious thought, their sick war against me, or death now. My kidneys are failing … my health is but a memory. Yet … I'm peacefully awaiting that door out still seeking people with eyes of light. Simply talking with you is as a blessing to me, my Indian friend. And because you are a rare man, a man of power and heart, a shaman who will help, that I know and believe just by talking with you. You are a compassionate man yet with a ruthless intellect. You remind me of a forgotten memory..." And then she said to my eyes, "May I call upon you again, Dan?"

I stood, embraced that sweet, fragile, feminine, immensely magnificent artist and smiling directly into her heart answered, "Of course, my friend. Of course you can and whenever you want." I then added, "I'm Piscean like your father. And I feel his presence here, now. I am and will be at your service if you need to bridge to me." We kissed; and smiling at me, Jan Kerouac slowly turned and vanished into the throng of selfish, oblivious, personal mirror-gazing energy-drainers strewn on her path walking light as a feather.

Recollecting absolutely all of this, our first interlude, a few months later, while standing at the very back of the stage at Fort Mason in San Francisco, against a brick wall, listening to her verse there in the Cowell Theatre, where a benefit show was being staged in her behalf, I felt again the presence of the Lowell football player standing next to me. This time I heard his words:

"That's my baby chanting her songs. Can you hear her?"

Turning to my left, there in the darkness at the rear of the stage, I nodded to ole Pisces Jack and whispered, "Yeah, man. I do ...," and we both laid back into that cool wall listening to her cool words.

Jan Kerouac had finished her reading. She stood in the spotlight as this was her night before the crowd and the applause. Dazzling bright lights dancing all around her, I saw her gently and with style turn her head and stare into the darkness at the rear of the stage. After a few moments, she broke into a great smile as if recognizing someone or something, lingered for an infinitude, enraptured, nodding in understanding of the portent she had beheld. A great shining light came from her. She was an *estrella* — a star.

Then she left the stage to join with her father, ole Pisces Jack, to finally be embraced and loved forevermore.

Gerald Nicosia

WHAT SHE INTENDED:
A RECOLLECTION OF JAN KEROUAC'S
YEARS OF WORK ON *PARROT FEVER*

In rereading the manuscript of *Parrot Fever*, I was struck more than ever by what an accomplished book it is—though clearly still only a work-in-progress. In the story of the two half-sisters, Maxine and Claire, there is no mistaking the harrowing but glorious life that was Jan Kerouac's. The ability to put such a stamp of originality on one's own life—to create a vision of it that no one else could steal or plagiarize if they wanted to, because it is so uniquely one's own—is the mark of a true writer.

I first heard of the rudimentary plan for *Parrot Fever* when Jan phoned me from her home in Ellensburg, Washington, in August, 1981. Like all of Jan's books, this one changed titles a number of times, and she was calling the book something else then, though I don't remember what. Her first novel, *Baby Driver*, was just about to be published, and Jan claimed that she had already started the second one. She made it very clear that she wanted to create some distance from the raw autobiography of *Baby Driver*, and she was thinking of including some of her past incarnations—which she truly believed in—as a means of doing so. "The book will end in India in 1990," she told me.

"Are you predicting your own future?" I asked, somewhat irritated with her. It sounded like the book was an excuse for further excessive globe-trotting or amorous adventures, and I was dismayed by what seemed her insatiable appetite for both. No doubt my own brief, unhappy romantic fling with Jan ("You're not my type—you're too kind," she said at one point) played some part in my disenchantment with this idea for a second novel. But the truth is, by this point I had willingly switched from the role of suitor to father-figure for Jan, and I was trying very hard to get her to settle down into a stable lifestyle and a productive work-routine. I knew that she could do great things with her life, but not if she kept chasing abusive, empty-headed hunks and will-o'-the-wisp crackpot invitations all over the planet.

"Oh no!" she assured me. She said she would not need to go to India, because she had already read many books about it and talked to many Indian people. She simply wanted to force her imagination to work harder as a means of getting free of slavishly recording her own life.

When I met her in San Francisco in July, 1985, she was already well along on writing her next novel, but it was not the one she had spoken of from Ellensburg in 1981. This was the book that would become *Trainsong*, which at that point she was calling *Loverbs*. I regretted to hear that she was back to autobiography. As per her editor's request, *Loverbs* (*Trainsong*) was going to be "a diary of all her relationships with men" over the past ten years, and was going to rely heavily for material on her new celebrity life—of money, world travels, and men, men, men—after the publication of *Baby Driver*. The most promising thing Jan told me during that visit was that she hadn't given up on the novel about her incarnations. She had sketched out the plot, she said, and would get back to it after she finished the sequel to *Baby Driver*.

When I heard from Jan in the spring of 1992, after having lost contact with her for almost two years, she had crossed several major watersheds in her life. The biggest one, of course, was the complete kidney failure she had suffered in Puerto Rico in January, 1991. She was now forced to do peritoneal dialysis four times a day—which she performed with her own IV equipment, bags of a special fluid that she had to order by the case, and a permanent catheter that had been implanted in her abdomen—to stay alive. She was living by herself in Albuquerque, and told me she had come to several major realizations about her life. The first was about men. She had reconciled herself to the fact that she was never going to have a life-partner, she said. She had always dreamed that she and her first husband John Lash would get back together, but he was now living in Europe with a French woman that he claimed was the love of his life. Jan said she did not want any more of her famous one-night stands or disastrous affairs with brutal criminals or compulsive womanizers. To avoid her weakness for the wrong kind of man, she was going to attempt to remain celibate for the rest of her life. The other main thing she talked about was her coming death.

First, though, she told me about her mother's death on May 15, 1990. It had occurred two days after Mother's Day, though soon she would be telling people that it had occurred on Mother's Day, and eventually she even seemed to believe that herself, getting the dates confused in various drafts of *Parrot Fever*. There is no question, however, that this was the most momentous event in her life outside of the death of her father, Jack Kerouac. Her mother had been her one true friend, her confidante, and the one person who would always offer her a home, food, and loving care whenever she needed it. When Joan died, Jan was orphaned in the most profound sense. She talked of how her mother had always been too proud and independent to accept other people's help, and had even refused to go to the hospital, until she was so sick that she had had to be taken there a few days before she died. Jan foresaw that she was going to need help in the future too. Though it went against her grain, Jan said she would accept it more cheerfully and gratefully than her mother.

Jan told me that the only thing that would save her life would be a kidney transplant, but she doubted that with the blood disease she'd inherited from her father (in her case, the blood didn't clot properly) she would be eligible for one. Also, she'd heard and read about the agonies of preparation and post-operative care that a kidney transplant entailed, and she was "leery," she said, of putting herself through such an ordeal. Instead, she had made peace with her shortened lifespan, and wanted to do the most important work she could in the little time left her. Primarily, she said, she wanted to finish her third novel.

Already, though, she admitted that the odds were against her. She had money to live now, thanks to the percentage of her father's royalties the Sampas family had been legally compelled to pay her, but the kidney failure was having a negative impact on almost all areas of her life—including other bodily functions. Her eyesight had deteriorated drastically, she could hardly feel in her fingers, her energy level was very low because of the continual interruption of her sleep for dialyses, her memory was getting spotty, and even her equilibrium was affected. "I stagger like a drunk and I'm not even drinking!" she laughed, for she still had her sense of humor about all this misfortune. As a result, she was no longer able to drive, and stayed home most of the time, ordering out for food and channel-surfing through the night, till it was time for her morning dialysis. "I live like a monk," she said, sounding sad and lonely. Completing her third novel, she said, was the only thing she really had to look forward to.

She was calling it alternately *Parrot Fever* and *Fired From Paradise*—not yet sure which title she preferred. It was clear that she was somewhat torn about which way to go with it. She wanted to keep it in the third person—except for the interposition of first-person "letters" from the protagonists—to attain the objectivity she had long sought in her fiction, and long been criticized for lacking. But the "incarnations" had been too much of a reach for her. Instead, she had settled for splitting herself into two separate main characters, the two half-sisters Claire and Maxine, and allowing her personality to be explored and analyzed through the interaction of the two. The big problem for her as a writer was to decide between letting the book simply become a sequel to the other two—the third and capping book in a trilogy—or giving free rein to her imagination to take it in an entirely different direction, permitting consequences and conclusions to enter the book that might not actually have happened in her life—at least not yet. For one thing, she wanted the more self-destructive of the two, Maxine, to die or disappear near the end. But it was apparent that she was already having trouble keeping the sisters separate both in her writing and in her head—a result, I think, of the strong autobiographical pull that always gripped Jan when she sat down to write. She would even mix up Claire's last name—at times in the manuscript she is Claire Haggerty, and at others she is Claire Luna, taking the last name of the novel's major male character, Jacob Luna. At several points in the writing of the book, Jan confided to me that her instinct was actually to make Jacob the main character. When she would say that, I always remembered how she'd once told me that most of her previous incarnations were as men—that her soul was male.

Interestingly, Jan said that one of the things that had motivated her to return to the book after her kidney failure was watching a TV documentary about scriptwriter Waldo Salt and, the same day, a TV showing of Salt's film *Midnight Cowboy,* one of her favorites. The scene of Dustin Hoffman's character, Ratso, dying before he ever reaches Florida touched her now more than ever, she said. At one point in her novel, Jan even quotes some of Ratso's dialogue. But what amazed her was to learn that Salt had spent decades trying to make it as a scriptwriter—writing many mediocre films such as *Taras Bulba*—before he authored masterpieces such as *Midnight Cowboy* and *Coming Home*, for which he won Oscars. Jan felt that if Waldo Salt could make a stunning breakthrough after decades of trying to get a handle on his art, perhaps she could do the same with *Parrot Fever.*

Almost every time we talked on the phone, her progress and problems with *Parrot Fever* were part of our discussions, and we also corresponded extensively about the book By the summer of 1992, Jan had already circulated sample chapters to several publishers, but had gotten rejections everywhere. She was discouraged, and felt that if she could get a contract for the book, not to mention a monetary advance, it would help inspire her to complete it—a task that grew increasingly hard as time passed and she grew physically weaker and more forgetful. To help her out, in October, 1992, I agreed to serve as literary agent for the book. I sent it to dozens of publishers—including Viking Penguin, now her father's main publisher—but again it was universally rejected. I would have been discouraged myself, had I not remembered the two years I'd spent submitting *Baby Driver* to every editor and publisher I could think of and seeing it too rejected over and over, until the combination of real literary agent Joyce Cole and St. Martin's Press editor Barbara Anderson made the book a reality. Of course *Parrot Fever* lacks the sort of titillating sex scenes that helped make *Baby Driver* a commercial success—the kind of scenes that—as Jan mocks in the new novel—people had come to expect her to write, so that they could get their cheap thrills from a safe distance, while pretending to admire her "courageous" life.

In 1994, Jan began the lawsuit against the Sampas family, aimed at recovering and preserving her father's literary archive, which consumed the last two years of her life. Both her medical and legal expenses were increasing rapidly, and her royalty income, which the Sampases sought to reduce, no longer covered all her needs. To raise needed money, Jan agreed to let printer Norman Davis issue a chapbook of selections from *Parrot Fever* that spring. I agreed to write the introduction, and to prepare myself for that, I had many discussions with Jan about where she was going with the book.

What I learned was that Jan had a very thorough, elaborate structure in mind for *Parrot Fever,* and that she really wanted the two sisters to be definite, separate characters whose interaction would resolve both the plot and the central mystery of the book—which is: why do gifted, intelligent people self-destruct in this world? The reader has to understand that Jan began this book—at least the real page-by-page writing of it, which she started around 1988—from the premise of a wrecked life. At this point, her health had already begun to fail, although she obviously had no idea how catastrophic that failure would become. I remember when she arrived in Lowell in June, 1988, for the dedication of the memorial to her father, her legs were swollen from the bus ride and she had other health problems that she thought at the time might be lupus, a disease her mother supposedly suffered from. She had broken up with her last serious lover, Michael in Boulder, three years earlier, and she no longer believed she would find a lifetime partner—as she told Lowell literary historian Brad Parker quite clearly.

When we talked about the book in 1994, Jan told me that she hoped the third-person point of view and dual heroines would allow her to get far enough outside herself to finally analyze how she had landed in such a mess, and to provide her with a useful perspective on her life and perhaps some peace of mind, if not actual hope for the future. She saw her life seesawing between two powerful magnetic poles—on the one hand, her desperate desire to preserve the joy, playfulness, and innocence of childhood; and on the other, her inability to meet the serious demands of the adult world, which kept pulling her into complex, usually tragic situations that she was ill-prepared to deal with. To put it as succinctly as possible, the central issue of the book is: where does childishness leave off and self-destruction begin?

Jan believed her lack of a father figure played a huge role in her inability to solve this dilemma, which most people get past with far less pain and suffering as they embark upon the mature portion of their lives. But she wanted *Parrot Fever* to get beyond just the simplistic bitching about daddy's absence that had characterized the two earlier books. She wanted this one—her masterpiece, she hoped—to become an allegory for the fractured psyche of everyman and everywoman, if not the fractured psyche of the world itself—and an allegory, even more important, of how that fracture can finally be healed. To this end, the two fatherless sisters' love and concern for each other was to play a key role in the plot. One of crucial scenes that never got written was that of Claire, the younger "emotional" one (as Jan called her), going to Hawaii near the end to search for her lost and possibly dead sister Maxine. At the end, the older sister, a successful writer who was supposed to have her life together, would crash even worse than Claire, "the family goof" and "profoundly disturbed dreamer" (again, these were terms with which Jan described her to me). The reversal of their usual roles was to comment on the human capacity for growth, in both good and bad directions. But she also wanted to show love as the glue that holds crumbling human life together. One of the central images—which also never found its way into the manuscript, at least the portion of it we have (and a considerable part was lost in Jan's move to Key West in 1993)—was to have been the poster for the movie *Ben Hur*. Jan told me that she used to stare fascinated at this poster when she was a child, and she loved the way BEN HUR was printed in big rocky crumbling letters. But Maxine, by keeping her mind fixed on those crumbling letters, and imagining that she will write a book that will become such an epic masterpiece, manages to put her life back together, at least in words on the page—much as Jan was trying to do with *Parrot Fever*. Thus artistic vision would serve as another glue for human life, working side by side with love.

I was awed by the ambitiousness of Jan's vision, and it was a major tragedy—both for her personally, as well as us, her friends and readers—that she never lived to realize it. What we have in *Parrot Fever*—marred by incomplete chapters, missing chapters, gaps where material was either lost or never written—is far smaller in scope, but like the stone skeleton of Jack London's burned-out Wolf House, it is still a remarkable piece of architecture. In even these shards of *Parrot Fever,* you can hear what was to have been Jan's *Moonlight Sonata*—sadness and passion and ominousness all mixed together. The promiscuous sex is still here, to a degree, but now the overtones are much darker than in *Baby Driver* or *Trainsong*. Sex becomes not an exciting adventure and pastime, as in the previous two novels, but rather an additional and deadly source of psychic and social fracture. There are dark references to the letdown and betrayal both sisters feel from their ex-husbands; and in the end, Claire seeks to end her desperate loneliness with a guy, Louie, whom she knows from the start is nothing but a sleazeball hustler. How ironic that Jan's first biographer, James Jones—whom she repudiated before his book came out—sought to emphasize her wild sex and "playgirl" life as somehow the essence of her character, when Jan herself had already moved far beyond those things, both in her life and her writing.

Like the greatest English literature, thinking back especially to Shakespeare, *Parrot Fever* begins with something about to go profoundly wrong with the world and the accepted order of things. This, of course, was the basic story of Jan's life: a beautiful little girl is born to a husband and wife, only the husband (and now daddy) is nowhere around, in fact is running as far as he can get from the family he has just created—leaving wife and daughter to deal with the cataclysmic consequences of this rupture themselves. Jan opens her story with Maxine LaCrosse stumbling upon a flood in Maine, where she has gone to help celebrate the work of her famous writer dad. It's noteworthy that Jack Kerouac himself used the imagery of a flood in *Dr. Sax* to suggest a world gone out of control as the young Jackie Duluoz enters puberty—though Jan, as far as I know, never consciously sought to imitate her father's work. As Jan's book begins, the flood and fog are "deranging" people, driving them "slowly, quietly mad," and there is a hint that human beings might actually start to murder one another.

This apocalyptic atmosphere pervades the novel, and there are numerous references to the possible coming end of human life. In fact, she intended—with typical Jan pun-in-cheek humor—to title the final chapter, in which Claire goes in search of her lost sister Maxine, "Apocalypso." Of course Jan was approaching the very definite end of her own human life as she wrote all this, and a part of what she was doing was trying to see her own life in the greater human continuum—to merge the two. In so doing, she finds a great personal consolation. She has lost the unity of her own family, but, as she says in "Hedda's Garden" (a kind of perverse version of the Garden of Eden), she has managed to make "her old fond dream come true, of being at the Earth's Hearth"—having reconstituted and rejoined the Family of Man.

Fortunately Jan did complete the book's two most important chapters, "Chernobyl Swan" and "Trainsong Park"—both of which I think are some of the finest short pieces of fiction written by any American writer in the last decade of the twentieth century. Throughout the book, Jan has been expounding upon her naïve, youthful idea that she can avoid becoming part of the world's evil by simply remaining a child-like witness to human life — like one of those people on the subway with their heads buried in the newspaper, riding home or to their job as they read of nuclear disaster in faraway Russia. But in "Chernobyl Swan," Claire finds that the witness cannot help becoming part of the evil machinery herself. She cracks open a swan's egg, wanting to see what she expects will be a dead embryo — killed by a fierce, possibly radioactive rainstorm in the wake of the nuclear power plant accident in Chernobyl. But the embryo was still alive; and in seeking to examine it, she kills it herself. "She felt as though she had committed a terrible crime by opening the egg and yet at the same time she knew that it would have died in there anyway," Jan writes, somehow condensing her whole life into that one brilliant image. If she had done nothing with her traumatized life, Jan would have died anyway; but in seeking to lead a full, adventuresome, creative human life, she has ironically hastened her own death.

That chapter, "Chernobyl Swan," incidentally, contains some of the most evocative writing about New York City that I think any American writer has ever done — an accomplishment which alone would make Jan Kerouac a significant writer.

"Trainsong Park" recounts the actual death of Jan's mother Joan Haverty in 1990. It rivals, in power and intensity, the great scene in her second novel *Trainsong*, where she meditates on her father's death at Allen Ginsberg's house in Boulder, Colorado, on October 21, 1982. In "Trainsong Park," Jan attempts to look at death head-on, and to see what it really means. Her mother is supposedly "gone," but "where had she gone?" Jan asks. Memories of her dominate Jan's consciousness, and she is still tremendously alive to Jan. But the big thing that is missing is Joan's distinctive voice. Death, Jan finds, is the Big Silence. Joan's children can now romp through her house, opening forbidden drawers, without fear of Joan yelling at them to stop, and it makes them feel "sheepish," as if "they had done something bad" by usurping what should have been her right to control her own home. Joan had been an immensely strong woman, seemingly able to overcome every form of human adversity, but somehow she has failed to surmount the worst human problem of all: death. "You can't just make a mistake like this and just fail," Jan says plaintively to the mother who is still in her head. In the futility of the children trying to do something useful with what she has left behind—even the Salvation Army rejects her dilapidated furniture—Jan makes a poignant comment on how helpless we all are before this final human destroyer, silencer, and leveler.

In the exceedingly hot summer of 1995, Jan moved to San Anselmo, California, a few miles from me. That whole summer, she had a blackish purplish sore on the top of her right foot the size of a nickel, which caused her extreme pain, and made it almost impossible for her to walk more than a few yards without stopping for relief. Needless to say, she wasn't traveling anywhere that summer, and even riding the bus became a virtual impossibility. So I drove to her house several times a week and took her to the grocery store, to the drugstore for bandages and salves, to the laundromat, and usually, at the end of her round of errands, to a coffeeshop or restaurant to relax for an hour or so—before she returned home to continue work on the novel in her sweltering house. It was in those dozens of different coffeeshops and restaurants that summer—as well as sometimes her famous late-night phone calls—that I heard her final plans for completing *Parrot Fever*.

One of the most exciting things to me were the scenes Jan projected that would for the first time deeply explore her relationships with men. One such key scene was to be a description of Claire's striptease act in a sleazy Eugene, Oregon, topless club—to be based upon Jan's own striptease act in such a place shortly before she left for Puerto Rico and her near-fatal kidney failure. Jan told me the scene would involve a confession of how she actually enjoyed stripping. "You get a whole stage and music and can do with it anything you want," she said. She had approached it in a creative fashion, devising all sorts of imaginative costumes and dance routines, many of which involved the black star-on-thigh tattoo her first real love, Paul Ortloff, had given her at about age twelve. What would give tension and clarity to the scene would be the contrast between what Claire expected—which was to receive loving adoration and appreciation from the men she danced for—and what she actually got: "a bunch of horny dolts who all wanted her to get down to the nitty-gritty, to see her naked." The scene, Jan said, would be a paradigm of her life: her search for love, repeatedly frustrated by men who only saw the hot, foxy sex symbol—the *Marilyn Monroe* that Claire wants so badly to become in one of the early chapters of *Parrot*

Fever—and not the lonely, unloved girl inside. Jan conveyed this cruel insensitivity in an image I liked so much at the time that I wrote it down in my notebook: "men [at the strip club] would look up at her [Jan/ Claire] with eyes demonically white and milky in the black light."

Another scene, also based on Jan's own life, would be one of the girls—probably Maxine, whose character needed beefing up—riding a Manhattan bus with her mother at about age two. The little girl lifts up her skirt to show off her new panties—knowing how cute she is—and embarrasses her mother. All the people smile at her mother to show their appreciation for her cute little girl. "They're really smiling for the mother," Jan said, "but the little girl thinks they're smiling at her." And the little girl quickly develops a craving for this kind of "outpouring of affection"—which, according to Jan, was the only equivalent she could find for the father-love that did not exist for her.

There were also to have been detailed scenes of Claire's life with Louie, the Puerto Rican gigolo. Claire—again based on Jan's own experience with a similar man in Puerto Rico—would continually go out of her way to meet Louie's needs, but when she needed something basic, even something as essential as a ride to the hospital when her body was beginning to collapse, Louie would shrug her off, saying it was too much trouble. At some point Claire would have an illumina-tion of where this excessive need to cater to men had come from. Jan wanted to recount the real-life episode of spending an hour with her father in her tenement apartment when she was about ten. She said a "blue spark of recognition" had passed between their eyes, and she had seen how much hurt it had caused Jack, since he had been forced to turn away from her for the rest of the visit. She had decided at that moment that it was her job to protect men from being hurt. It was that moment, Jan claimed, that began her years of taking care of men who were "big babies," letting them abuse her and always blaming herself for their unhappiness.

Jan's mother was going to come in for some heavy criticism too—for the first time in her writing, though she often criticized her in private to me and other close friends. She wanted to show a scene of one of the girls—probably the same panty-flasher on the bus—wanting a hug and kiss from her mother, and being coldly rebuffed. In reality, Jan said, Joan almost never hugged her at all as a child, and she felt that such absence of physical affection may have done real emotional damage to her.

It seemed to me that what would make *Parrot Fever* so radically different from Jan's earlier books was this no-holds-barred approach, which would make everyone—her mother, her father, even her own self (or perhaps one should say *selves*)—fair game for critical analysis. In September, 1995, just before she returned to Albuquerque for the last time, Jan told me she wanted to recast the whole book from Jacob's point of view. Obviously she would soon fall far too sick to even begin such a massive revision, but there was a genuine artistic impulse at work in such a plan. She admitted that in seeing herself dissected in the two half-sisters, she disliked a lot of what she saw in her own personality and behavior. She found Jacob a much more sympathetic and likable character—the kind of person she wished she could have been. She had based a lot of the "Jacob" chapter on her interaction with her agent Peter Livingston, who later died of AIDS. In reality, she said, there had been a sordid side to that relationship too, as she had actually been having a secret love affair with Livingston despite the fact that he was married at the time.

I think if Jan could ever have really broken through all her protective facades and cover stories—as she at least suggested to me that she would do in *Parrot Fever*—she could have produced a truly great novel. She told me the novel would essentially have two morals or mantras. One would occur in a scene where one of the half-sisters sees a sexy, dreamy young woman swishing blithely by in her miniskirt in some café, unconscious of all the actual misery around her, and she thinks, "Just you wait, dearie, you'll find out what *pain* is all about." That mantra was a vision of the universal suffering that all flesh is heir to—on a par with Dostoyevsky. The other mantra would occur in a scene that I thought was an absolute stroke of genius—a scene between Claire and her mother in Sacred Heart Hospital in Eugene, just before Joan's death.

In one of her last utterances, Joan said, "Jan, you know I'm going to be all right, don't you?" Thinking her mother wanted to be comforted, Jan had answered, "Yes." When her mother died a few hours later, Jan was overcome by immense guilt for having lied to her. But eventually Jan—and this would be the key to the scene—came to see that what was actually transpiring was *Joan's attempt to comfort Jan*. That someone on the verge of death could think enough of someone else's needs to put that other person's comfort first was an astounding revelation to Jan. Although never conventionally religious, Jan was definitely seeking some form of religious or spiritual truth as she approached her own death, and Joan's final act of selflessness seemed like some ultimate form of salvation to Jan—something she could always look back to whenever she needed comfort in her own life, a gift that could never be taken away. The importance of caring for others was thus to be the book's other great lesson.

"Why did she want to title it *Parrot Fever*?" some people ask. The fact is Jan loved parrots—all birds, in fact—and, besides her relationship with the real-life Macadamia, had often kept parakeets for pets. But beyond that, I think she could find no better symbol for the essential message of her book than the parrot. It is a benevolent, human-friendly, fun, childlike creature—but it is also the bearer of a potentially fatal disease. That paradox is at the heart of the book's double vision. The small, lithe, ever-curious and quirky green parrot is a symbol of Jan herself—or at least a significant part of her nature—and the disease she tries to avoid is mortality. She tries to avoid it by becoming an expert observer and chronicler of it, but in the end that isn't enough to save her from the universal, fatal contamination. Yet she manages to make friends with the parrot's disturbing behavior and even its destructiveness—learns to make peace with its troublesome intrusions and even to soothe its mad flurries with her own love songs—as Jacob eventually makes friends with Mackie and plays classical piano compositions such as *Les Oiseaux Tristes* for her. That is how I think of *Parrot Fever*—as Jan's final love song to her own troublesome life.

Gerald Nicosia

INTERVIEW WITH JAN KEROUAC

I made the following interview with Jan Kerouac on June 4, 1979, at my home in Lyons, Illinois. Two days earlier, I had introduced Jan at the national convention of the National Society of Arts and Letters at the Ritz-Carlton Hotel in Chicago, and an editor at the *Chicago Sun-Times* had assigned me to do the interview with her. She had come down from Ellensburg, Washington, to stay with me for a couple of weeks, during which time I was doing everything possible to boost her career. She was working on her first novel during that period, still called *Everthreads*, and from time to time she would grow despondent and consider giving it up. The recognition she had received at the NSAL convention buoyed her considerably, and you can hear in the interview her renewed sense of confidence that her novel was destined to be published. In fact, it would be published a little over two years later, as *Baby Driver*, by St. Martin's Press.

I lived in the garret on the top floor of the house, and the night we did the interview was hot and sticky. Only a small window looking out on Custer Avenue let in the hint of a breeze. Jan and I sat on the sofa together, with the tape recorder in front of us. John Coltrane, her dad's favorite musician (at least at the end of his life), set the tone on the stereo. Earlier, Jan had sent me to the local liquor store for a fifth of Kahlua, and we drank her favorite white Russians throughout the interview—which as I recall, went on for hours. Jan did not show much sign of getting drunk. For a hundred-pound waif of a girl, she could hold her liquor remarkably well. Only near the very end, her speech slurred a bit and she occasionally stumbled over a word. In characteristic fashion, she makes a linguistic joke of one such stumble—turning it into "happity in povery," her description of her mental state in childhood.

For me, the key moment in the interview came when I related something that her mother had told me a year earlier: that Jan "fell apart inside" at the news of her father's death. Jan reacted with real shock to that revelation. You had to have been there to know how stunned she looked—and how loudly and almost angrily she demanded, "She did???" It was clear that Jan had absolutely never considered such a possibility before, and even more apparent that she did not want me thrusting such a possibility—a veritable black pit of despair at the center of her life—in front of her in what had started out as a friendly interview. What followed, her hurried insistence that her father's death had actually made her stronger, was transparently a case of "the lady protesting too much," and I think Jan knew it herself. But in some sense, I think the rest of her life was at least partly an attempt to solve that enigma that I'd perhaps too casually dropped in her lap—without my even realizing the force those words would hit her with, or the extent of what they were asking her to realize about herself.

We stopped the interview when we ran out of tape—that is why it ends so abruptly as Jan is talking about, and ridiculing, my hometown of Chicago. We stayed up for a long time after that, still drinking, and I played her a long tape of her dad singing popular jazz songs with backup musicians at his friend Jerry Newman's recording studio. Jack had a decent voice, but was drunk himself and pretty maudlin as he sang his favorite Sinatra tunes. I'll always remember the glazed, sated look in her eyes as she lay back in an overstuffed chair listening to her dad wail Sinatra classics like "In the Wee Small Hours of the Morning," "I Get Along Without You Very Well," and "Come Rain or Come Shine." The glaze wasn't just from all the alcohol she'd drunk. "His voice is like a lullaby to me," she said. I was grateful to finally be able to play that lullaby for her.

GN: When you were growing up, when you first came to awareness of yourself as a little child, your father wasn't living with you. When did you first remember hearing who your father was?

JK: It was way back. It seems ever since I can remember, I dimly knew who my father was, because my mother talked about him—especially when we came back from Missouri. Well, that's kind of a long story, but at first I was about to be adopted by this stepfather of mine, but it never happened. I was about to become acquainted with the name Aly, as my name—and I was just about to think that this was going to be my name for the rest of my life—when my mother left this Aly character, and she told me, "Well, now it looks like your name is going to be Kerouac, like it ought to be." And so there was a big to-do about learning how to spell my real name—which was pretty complicated—and I remember going through the process of learning how to spell it, when I was about eight, and feeling very proud of it. It wasn't my mother's name either. It was just my name, and my father's name.

GN: Did your mother tell you who your father was or describe him to you? Or say anything about why he wasn't there?

JK: I can't remember all the details about that, and I was very young. Later on, after I was nine, I learned gradually more and more about him because I asked about him, and by the time I was nine or ten I knew almost all there was to know about him as far as who he was and how come he wasn't around and things like that.

GN: Why did your mother say he wasn't around?

JK: Well, because they'd separated, and they didn't get along as well as they thought they might—and that when I had been a baby and before I was even born, they split up for reasons of incompatibility, which seemed easy enough for me to understand.

GN: Did you have a lot of curiosity about your father? Did you want to meet him?

JK: Yeah, I wanted to meet him, and when I finally did meet him, I was very excited—and I identified with him when I met him. He seemed to be sort of a larger version of myself—and I was very proud of him. I felt almost as if I had created him, instead of vice versa.

GN: Recapitulate briefly how you met him.

JK: I was never that interested in the legal hassles that my mother was undergoing with him, and I always sort of viewed them as being unnecessary, 'cause I didn't really care if I got support checks from him. I just wanted to meet him. But now I understand why it was she wanted support checks. It had something to do with a paternity test to see if I was really his daughter—a blood test—and my mother's lawyer … his lawyer was Eugene Brooks, Allen Ginsberg's brother—that's all I know—I don't think my mother had a lawyer. But we met him out in Brooklyn somewhere with his lawyer, and we went walking along the street, and I remember looking at this character who was my father, and feeling very interested in him. The first thing I remember him doing was suggesting we go to a bar, for lunch, instead of to a restaurant, and I thought it was kind of cute, because it shocked his lawyer. His lawyer was making all kinds of objections. He said, "This little daughter shouldn't have to go to a bar," but I'd been in millions of bars already living in the Lower East Side—with all my weirdo father images—so it didn't shock me in the least. In fact, I felt more at home in a bar. So we went into a bar. It was the day the astronauts went up in space—around 1960 or '61.

GN: 1962—it was John Glenn orbiting the earth.

JK: And I remember the TV set up in the corner of the ceiling was blaring with white-and-black images of astronauts as we sat there. My mother and father reminisced about their early life together, and I looked back and forth between them, and felt for the first time a certain wholeness. I always had suspicions that I was a real human being with two parents, and now it was being confirmed.

GN: Did you know the reason for the paternity suit, that your father was denying that you were his child? And were you puzzled or did you wonder why?

JK: I can remember my mother telling me that the whole problem was that he had told his mother that I wasn't his daughter way in the beginning, to protect his mother, who was kind of a hysterical type—and had just been worried that someone was trying to bother her precious son, and he consoled her and told her that no, it wasn't true, that he didn't really have a daughter. But he couldn't go back on this lie that he told his mother, and so he sort of talked himself into a corner and didn't know how to get out of it. But I figured that that wasn't his biggest problem anyway. I never really felt like my being his daughter was of primary importance somehow. I know it may sound like I'm just saying that or something, but I've never really felt resentment for him, for his not paying attention to me—because even when I was very young, I kind of understood that he was doing something more important—something very important—that he sacrificed fatherhood for something grander. I knew he was out there bumbling around in some kind of very important universe.

GN: You knew he was a writer?

JK: Yeah, I knew that. Well, I knew all there really was to know about him, as far anyone could tell me, like my mother.

GN: Did you have a conception of what a writer was? I mean, did you read a lot of books in those days?

JK: I was just beginning to read. I was in the fourth grade, and I was reading these strange little books. I had a binge where I was reading books about lions in Africa—I don't know who they were by or anything. I got them out of the library. It was always from the lion's point of view, and how it was to be a lion—and kill zebras and eat them in Africa.

GN: Did a writer seem like a hero to you, like a cowboy or something?

JK: No. I had this vague concept of the Beats, I suppose, as being these older people.

GN: You knew about the Beats?

JK: Well, I knew that all the people that my mother knew were in a certain category. They were hipsters. That's sort of what I thought of him as.

GN: You knew that word when you were nine or ten?

JK: It was used all around me from a certain crowd of people on the Lower East Side who were different from so-called straight people, and I felt sort of proud to have my parents, my elders, belong to that crowd. Like we were somehow special or something.

GN: How did you know what straight people were like?

JK: Because I saw them all the time. They lived in Stuyvesant Town. In my little tiny world, Stuyvesant Town was this project on 14th Street, to the north of my neighborhood, and I knew that those were straight people—they were the parents of the children who I went to school with.

GN: Did you know that your father was called "the King of the Beats"?

JK: Yeah, I was told that several times—it sunk into me pretty well.

GN: Did it impress you that your father was a king?

JK: Yeah, it must have been somehow impressive. I mean, I know it was. It's very hard to go back and actually take these little feelings apart, and try and decide exactly how important they were, because all these things are sort of dissolved since then. Well, they're not really dissolved—because they're there somewhere, but their impact is sort of dissolved. But, yeah, I know that must have been important to know that.

GN: So when you met him, he lived up to all your feelings about him and more?

JK: Now that I look back on it, I can't remember what my expectations were precisely, before I met him, because you know there's a very thin line there. When I did meet him, I remember, the main thing about him was that I thought he was very handsome, and I felt a certain strange pride that might have been almost like the type of pride that a parent would have for a child. I felt sort of as if I had created him—now that I think about it—and I felt sort of proud of him. I thought, Oh! So this is my father! He's cute! You know, 'cause I saw him staggering around the street and acting like a real noodlebrain! Just as I figured any father of mine would act.

GN: Why do you say that? Did you think you were a noodlebrain?

JK: I say that reveringly. I have always had a certain concept of myself as a noodlebrain. I don't know how to describe that. Anyway, he had a way of talking that I recognized as being similar to my way of talking, immediately when I heard it.

GN: How did he react to you?

JK: Oh yeah, that's another story. He acted like a shy young boy on his first date. That's what I thought, because I'd already had some boyfriends, not really serious boyfriends yet, but just sort of smooching boyfriends, like Puerto Ricans that would come see me and we'd stand around the doorway by the park or something, and so I had some concept of what guys were like and how they acted, when they were young, and I knew ... yeah, he acted as though he wasn't sure how he should react to me, and I felt sort of the same about him, because we'd both heard a lot about each other, and finally we were meeting.

GN: Did you feel loved? I mean, did you feel any love emanating from him?

JK: If it was, it was very filtered and coming from a very far-away inner spring, you know?

GN: Did you want to be loved by him?

JK: Well, you know, that's the kind of question that is so ... that goes so subconscious. I can't really say ... of course, I must have, but I can't really pinpoint the actual feeling and talk about it, because it's so far beneath all the other things. The main thing that I remember consciously feeling is that I wanted to be his friend, his buddy—that I wanted to feel a kind of camaraderie with him. And I did feel that, and I looked at his way of relating to my mother with a kind of awe and curiosity—as they were sitting in a bar there, and I was eating this hamburger that I was supposed to be eating because I was a kid, and I wasn't supposed to be in the bar in the first place. It was all the lawyer's idea, so I shouldn't be shocked, which was a joke, because I'd spent most of my life in bars already. They were drinking beer or something. I remember him saying to my mother, "You always used to burn the bacon," and things like that—very mundane little memories, and she would laugh and say a few other things to him about something that he used to do, and this was all during the period where he was typing *On the Road,* I guess, and I was in the womb. And it was just really amazing to hear these real episodes that went on while I was in the womb, and these little chiding comments that they gave each other. It really just made me feel like I was a real human being to listen to them, because I had little friends who had mothers and fathers—and I'd always just had a mother with a father as a kind of a legendary figure out in the universe, and now I saw them both together. It was like two halves of something coming together—nice.

GN: So you had your blood tests together?

JK: Yeah. Of course, all of this is in that little story that I wrote, called "B Flat." After we finished sitting around at the bar, we all went to some kind of a clinic—where Jack and I had blood tests. And it may seem funny to call him "Jack," but I really like that name—and I like calling him "Jack" just as well as I like calling him "my father." So anyway, we all went to this clinic to have our blood tested, and I had this feeling that there was some substance in our blood, just Jack's and my blood, that no one else had in the world, and that they needed it for some special experiment. You know these notions that one gets when one's very young.

GN: After the blood test, Jack came up to the room, or did you take him to the liquor store first?

JK: What happened was that first we met on the street somewhere, walking along, and this is how I remember it. It might have been quite different. I'm always telling my mother these stories, and she's constantly correcting me, but this is basically how it happened. We went to the bar—and they were drinking, and I was having a hamburger and crap like Seven-Up or something, and after that we went to the clinic and had our blood tested. And it wasn't determined right there, but I knew, I had no shadow of a doubt in my mind that he wasn't my father. It was just obvious to me, and I know it was obvious to him too. But in his haze he just kind of chose not to acknowledge it, and I understood. I just understood that little thing that happened—that little secret about what he told his mother—but I just didn't think it was that important to bring it out in the open, because I knew he knew it anyway. So why make a big deal about it? Because he obviously didn't want to go into a big thing. He had other things on his mind. Then what happened was we went back to my neighborhood—that was really funny. I mean, that was the highlight of the whole thing, because he came to our apartment, and the first thing he wanted was to go to the liquor store, around the corner. I led him there very proudly, because this was my father, you know, and nobody else had ever seen my father before, and nobody knew I had one. Of course, they probably thought it was just some old, anonymous guy that I was walking along with. But I didn't care, because I knew it was my father.

So I took him to the liquor store on 10th Street, and he got a bottle of Harvey's Bristol Cream Sherry. We didn't talk to each other much on the way, because he was sort of shy, and I didn't want to disturb him too much by talking. I felt like he was kind of precarious or something, and I didn't want to bother him too much. I figured I'd just let him go along at his own speed, but I was looking up at him kind of with curiosity and awe—just as I would with a shy boyfriend. That's always the way I was with boyfriends—I was always sort of very careful of them as if they were some kind of delicate thing that could be destroyed very easily or something. So I let him start all the conversations. Anyway, we went back up to the place, and he actually paid more attention to my sisters, my half sisters, than he did to me, which I was a little bit resentful of, but I didn't really blame it on him—'cause I knew it gave him a way, a vehicle, of avoiding the more serious question of me, 'cause he was probably kind of disturbed about meeting me—not knowing how to react—and so meeting my sisters gave him an outlet. They were very fascinated by him as they were with all the different guys that came over to the place. To them he was just another funny guy that came over to entertain them, just like certain junkies or alcoholics that always came over, but to me he was my special, my very own funny guy, because he was my father, and so he was more important to me somehow than he was to them, and I realized all this, and I just let them stay there and laugh at him as he drank his sherry and made little jokes. He was tearing off black plastic pieces of the bottle, and putting them down on the table, and we'd have a little piece of black plastic there, and he'd point at it and say, "Sheeesh a Russian! Sheesh no good! Sheesh a Russian." And I don't know where he got that from, but they erupted in peals of laughter, and it was very effective.

I just watched him and laughed and waited for him to say something to me, which he didn't do very often, but that didn't really bother me … it probably did bother me in a way, but my logic has always overruled my feelings—I mean, I always feel like whatever feelings I have are real, but logic always wins out in the end—'cause it seems a little more long-lasting. Emotions are like little flames that just flare up and they're gone the next day, so I don't pay too much attention to them, which may or may not be good. So he left, and he almost forgot his survival hat. He went out the door, and I was watching him go, and I must have known he was coming back, because when I looked at the door, I didn't feel this sensation of him leaving, and so I didn't look at the door as if, "Well, he's going now." I just sort of watched him go in a kind of daze, as if I knew he was about to come back any minute, and he did. He came back, and he said, "Whoops! I forgot my survival hat!" and we gave him his hat, and then he said, "Well, see ya in Janyary," and it seemed like the type of thing I might say. Funny … the only thing that I kept from that visit was the cork from this bottle—which every once in a while I'd take out and I'd look at it—until I lost it like everything else.

GN: Would you say that your father had a strong influence in the way that you grew up from that time on?

JK: Yeah, from that time on I was more realistically aware of the fact that he was my father, and so naturally I had more of an image of who my father was than I had before, and I was more curious about what he was doing. I talked to him on the phone once after that, maybe about a year later, maybe sooner, I don't remember.

GN: You had found his number and called him?

JK: Yeah! Somebody gave me his number, I'm not sure if it was Ginsberg.

GN: Lucien Carr said it was him.

JK: Oh him, that's right. I called him and talked to him for hours, it seemed, and he was drunk, and so he was talking very freely, and telling me all these things. He was telling me about the family crest, and referring to it as your, our, you know—acknowledging that it was mine also, probably because there was nobody else around, and so he didn't have to worry about anyone knowing that he was acknowledging that he was my father. But we knew it, so what the hell? And I'm sure he always knew it deepdown, but I understand this mentality that goes along with drinking. I've drunk a lot myself. I could perfectly imagine being him and making these little jokes about being sterile and stuff. It's just part of the whole alcohol mentality—not that that's all he had, 'cause of course he had quite a complex mentality, despite the alcohol.

GN: Were you ever curious to read his books at that time, 13 or 14?

JK: I never read anything, I never thought about his books at that time. For some reason, they just didn't seem available. I didn't come across them until I got hepatitis and went to Lincoln Hospital in the Bronx, 'cause I'd run away from home, which is a long story. Anyway, one morning I woke up and I had some kind of welts all over my body, and it turned out that I had to be taken to the hospital, which was a great holiday from the detention home, and so I was elated. And while I was there, there was a doctor—Dr. Bruckner—who was my doctor, and noticed my name and said, "Well, you ought to read *On the Road*," and he gave me a copy, and so while I was in there I read it. That was the first time I read *On the Road*. I've never been an extremely avid Kerouac reader because I just didn't feel like I had to. Naturally I come upon his works from a different direction than most people ... from underneath maybe.

GN: What was your impression of *On the Road*? Were you excited by it?

JK: It seemed very natural to me to be reading it, and I understood it. I was constantly aware of the fact that this doctor had sort of forced it on me, because I was his daughter and I should read it, and I kept thinking of that constantly as I read it, but at the same time I realized that it was worth reading. Later on, I read other things on my own, at my own speed. *Maggie Cassidy* was one I really identified with, because I was living in Santa Fe, New Mexico, with all these Chicanos in this very Catholic situation. Reading *Maggie Cassidy* about Jack's adolescence and his Catholic upbringing, I really identified with him.

GN: You still haven't read all his books?

JK: Oh no.

GN: More than half? Less than half?

JK: I read *On the Road*, I read *The Subterraneans* in London—when I was just beginning to write my book—also *Lonesome Traveler*, which is just about my favorite, and I've read snatches of *Doctor Sax* and pieces of *Visions of Cody*, but I can't think of any other books that I've read. But I *will* eventually read them.

GN: You don't have an overwhelming curiosity to read them?

JK: No, because where would I get such a curiosity?

GN: I mean, he's your father.

JK: I sort of feel like he's in my blood somewhere. I mean, there's all the time in the world to read them ... Let's see, how should I put this? Since I'm coming from ... I was gonna say, from behind the whole thing, but beneath it is probably a better description. I'm coming out of the fountain rather than finding it, stumbling on it, dying of thirst.

Since I feel like I already have all of his feelings, and his tendencies are already inside me, I'm not searching for them as if they were something outside of myself.

GN: You seem to me to have a very, very strong identification with your father—and yet you knew him so much less than most women would know their father.

JK: Yeah.

GN: I wonder if there's some correlation between the fact that you knew him in person so little and the fact that you have probably a much stronger identification with your father than most women do.

JK: Well, he never had a chance to reprimand me for anything! Maybe that has something to do with it—I don't know.

GN: Or maybe a desire to know him through yourself?

JK: Well that's the only way I could know him at this point. I really do feel like I wish—I mean, I know I wish I knew him. Wait a minute, let me start over again. I certainly wish I had had a chance to know him better. But in all honesty, I don't think I'm riddled with despair at his not having been more of a father to me, like most people expect me to be. Maybe subconsciously somewhere I have some deep-seated resentment or something, but I really doubt it, because I've really searched myself in dreams and everything. I really don't blame him for any of it. I just see it as fate, you know? The way it turned out. And I was brought up perfectly well by my mother, I figure, even though she wasn't a very conventional mother, probably because she wasn't a very conventional mother.

GN: My impression is that you sort of grew up on the street.

JK: Part of the time, yes. I won't go into the whole thing. But briefly, I was born in Albany, my mother was running around doing something— trying to find some babysitters for me. She was a waitress. I went through that period of infancy somehow, part of the time living with my Uncle Dave, who then went to the Army or something. My mother would probably have a fit if she heard me saying all this, because I probably have some of the details wrong—but that'll all come out later—but this's what I remember. I was often going to my grandmother's in Wappinger's Falls, New York, because my mother somehow would fail to be able to take care of me. It must have been pretty difficult all alone like that. Then we were living in uptown Manhattan, and my mother caught tuberculosis and she had to go to a TB hospital in Oneonta, New York. While she was there, I had to stay with my grandmother again in upstate New York—in a different place. She left the hospital after a few months—she couldn't stand it—and they really thought she wasnuts, and a lot of things happened. She walked out—in typical headstrong fashion—and went back to New York without anybody knowing about it, and met this guy where she was waitressing. This guy she ran into was my future stepfather. She somehow got pregnant by him, and then it turns out my grandmother wouldn't let her have me back unless she married this guy—which was kind of a dirty trick. So she had to marry this guy, and she didn't even like him! But she wanted to get me back. It was like blackmail in a certain respect. So she told her mother, "OK, I'll marry him," and she got me back. By that time, she had these twins—my sisters, Kathy and Sharon. And they were born in a New York hospital. Then we went down to New York City, which I was very excited about, because I've always had a real love for the city—and it always seemed to me like the ultimate excitement just to be in the city and live there. I'd always walked around with my mother, on the streets, in front of these shiny shop windows and everything, and smelling all these whiffs of hamburgers and carbon monoxide, and it has a lot of fond memories for me. So I went back to the city and lived in this tenement up on Amsterdam, which no longer exists. I think they built Lincoln Center where it was, and we lived there for a while. Then we went to Missouri with this guy, John Aly, this husband of hers, I mean my stepfather, or whatever he was. We went back with my twin sisters, because he considered that a woman should live in the man's home state, and he was from Missouri. He had this big father complex—and that's a long story. Anyway, we went to New Zealand, Missouri—and lived there for two years, until she got sick of him, and then, like the independent, wild Aries that she is, she suddenly decided to up and leave and we came back to New York. And that was also very exciting to me, 'cause I remember after two years of living in the Midwest, down there with silos and wheat fields and tornados and Baptists, we were suddenly coming back on the Continental Trailways bus and hearing Puerto Rican music approaching and getting stronger and stronger, and it seemed like we were coming back to life or something.

GN: Was all this before the paternity suit?

JK: Yeah, well, she had to have gotten divorced already; otherwise, she couldn't have married John Aly.

GN: She got divorced around '52, I think?

JK: Yeah, she went down to Juarez, Mexico, while she was pregnant with my twin sisters. I heard about that.

GN: She got Jack to sign something because she told him she wanted to marry somebody else. Then he agreed to a divorce.

JK: I seem to remember going through something similar once.

GN: You dropped out of school at a very early age, didn't you?

JK: Mm-hmm! Well, depends, not terribly early—ninth grade, if you consider that early ….

GN: Freshman year of high school would be considered pretty early.

JK: Yeah, for a while I was actually going to Hunter College Junior High School in Manhattan, which was really the height of my early school career. I was really happy about it. I was taking Latin and all kinds of interesting things—I was a straight-A student at that point, and then suddenly I started taking acid and getting involved in other things, and school just started to dissolve.

GN: What year was this?

JK: I'm not sure. February of '52 I was born.

GN: Freshman year of high school you would have been roughly fourteen.

JK: I think I was thirteen!

GN: 1965?

JK: Yeah! That was when I had my first acid trip.

GN: That's really when acid was becoming popular.

JK: Yeah. I took my first acid trip on February 14, 1965, which was two days before my thirteenth birthday ... Wait a minute! '65? That's right, that's right.

GN: You were in high school already?

JK: Actually I was in 7th grade, I had just gotten into Hunter—yeah! I was in this fabulous love affair with this tattoo artist that I had met, Paul Ortloff, who gave me a tattoo. But unfortunately he was 23, and I was 13, and my mother thought that was a bit old—a bit much of an age gap—and she was probably right in certain respects. She was trying to protect me, but I was too headstrong, and that was the beginning of my rebellion. I just didn't care what she thought—'cause all the other urges were much stronger, so I just went against her, and then all the Bellevue episodes ensued, and I got into all kinds of trouble, and ran away from home.

GN: This was after you dropped out of high school? Or you were in Bellevue before you dropped out of high school?

JK: OK, I was going along just fine, everything was just looking rosy. I had gone to seventh grade already, and then I started eighth grade— and right around December, I guess it was '65, I had a falling out with my mother. We were having mother-and-daughter problems, and so we got into this out-patient thing at Bellevue Hospital, and I was being really incorrigible. I don't blame her for doing whatever she did—because I just insisted on seeing this guy that I knew—and she refused to let me see him because she knew that was leading to disaster. And then I said, "Well, I'm going to keep seeing him," and she said, "Well, I'll call Bellevue, then"—just as a kind of a threat, you know. She didn't really mean it, but she had other kids to take care of—she already had my little brother at that point, too. He was just born, and I was being terribly difficult, but I didn't look at it in any other point of view than my own, and so I said, "Well, OK, call Bellevue, go ahead, do it." You know: "I don't believe you—that you'll call Bellevue." So she did. So I just sat there in the air shaft, smoking grass, and drinking brandy, and sure enough the Bellevue guys came! They arrived in their van, and they came up the stairs and walked into my room and said, "All right, what seems to be the problem?"—just like New York cops or whatever. And I was completely stoned out of my gourd, so I said, "Well, nothing's the problem." They got all my stuff together and said, "OK, come with us," and I poured all this junk that I had into this huge sack, irregardless of what shape or size it was—and went downstairs feeling sort of proud that I had actually gotten my mother to call them, and now I was showing her a thing or three! I felt like, "Well I am going to Bellevue! See what you've done!" And so I went to Bellevue, and the whole neighborhood was standing out on their stoops watching the spectacle of the evening, which happened to be the wagon coming to get me. And so I was taking my turn with the neighborhood scandal. Everyone else had done it so far, up and down the block.

GN: Is Bellevue a place for drug addicts?

JK: Bellevue is synonymous with nuthouse in New York City. The word Bellevue, you make jokes: "Ah, you oughtta go to Bellevue! ... Ho ho!"

GN: So it's not specifically drugs, then?

JK: NO! It's just a psychiatric hospital with a very bad reputation, and everybody goes to Bellevue when they're nuts, or that's how everybody looks at it. It's by the East River, around 21st Street, and it's very old. Well, they must have put on some new additions by now, but it's a very old psychiatric hospital.

GN: Did they run you through a lot of tests?

JK: Yeah, and I was really having a great time because I loved to play with the minds of psychiatrists anyway. And I was having a heyday because I could do anything I wanted, because I didn't care if I got admitted. In fact, I sorta hoped I would be. I did hope I would be—and I was drunk and stoned, and so I did everything in my power to get admitted. It was really a lot of fun. I could do whatever I wanted—and I did get admitted, I managed to do it. And it was all to show my mother—it was just stupid. Then the next few days she had to come and see me, and she was extremely sorry that I was put in. She didn't know what to do, and she was trying to get me out—you know, meanwhile trying to take care of all these other kids. And I had no concept of how difficult that was—just completely ignored it—like a true adolescent all wrapped up in my own affairs. I wound up staying there for a whole month, and instead of getting out at the end of that time, I was transferred to another hospital, Kings County Hospital, in Brooklyn.

GN: You were beaten up in Bellevue, didn't you tell me that?

JK: Well, no, in Kings County actually—by some disturbed adolescents. It was really a lot of fun when I was put in the women's ward, Q-6. Every Thursday night we had dances with the men's ward, which was fun—but then when I was inevitably transferred to the juvenile ward because of my age, everything went downhill, because juveniles had to show off all of their quirks. They weren't sure of themselves—and the dykes there were more obnoxious. Everything was more obnoxious—because all of their problems were just forming, and so it was really intolerable. When I finally got out of Kings County, my mother had this new set of rules for me to go by. I couldn't see anybody that was over 18, but I somehow managed to get by that—and went into an even worse period of shooting Methedrine, and doing all sorts of things, and it goes on and on. At this point things are getting more and more concentrated, up until fall of '67, when I finally just had to leave New York City, because I was pregnant. I saw Jack for the last time then too.

GN: When you were about to be arrested?

JK: Well, I had been in all kinds of trouble, and I was on probation from something else.

GN: And you were only fifteen years old?

JK: Yeah, I was only fifteen years old, and I was pregnant, and we realized—my mother and I ... at that point, she'd given up ... I haven't even gone into the fact that I went into the Youth House, this place in the Bronx that's since been exposed by a lot of people for some of the terrible things that went on there. It was an awful place.

GN: So you were in a position where you felt you had to leave the country? You knew you were gonna leave the country?

JK: Oh yes, because I was pregnant, and my mother even helped me with this, because the probation officers would take routine samples of urine to see if the girls were pregnant, and if they were, they'd send them right away to Hudson Girls Reformatory School, on the Hudson River, and they'd stay there till they were 21! Now we couldn't have that.

GN: Just for being pregnant?

JK: Just for being pregnant! They'd take the baby away when it was born and give it to a foster home, and then I'd go into a girl's reformatory with a whole bunch of dykes for six years, and that would be ... wonderful. We couldn't have that, so my mother had me bring a bottle of her own urine in to the probation officer. We switched the bottles. That way, they let me off probation, and we had this big yarn. My sisters had already been taken away by their father at this point, and they were out in Washington somewhere. My mother wanted to get over there to try and get them back, so we told them that we were all going to Washington. We were turning over a new leaf and all this—and so they let me off probation, on the basis that I was going to Washington, but I didn't go to Washington. I went to Mexico with my future husband, John Lash. And my mother wrote a notarized note saying he was a friend of the family, and I could go anywhere I wanted to with him, even though I was a minor—it was all right with her. And so first we went up to Lowell, Massachusetts, to see Jack for the last time, 'cause that's where he was living then in '67.

GN: So he was still a strong figure in your consciousness?

JK: Sure! I had to see him one more time. Oh, I didn't know it was going to be the last time, though.

GN: You hadn't seen him in all those years?

JK: I hadn't seen him since I was nine, right.

GN: But it was terribly important for you to see him at that time?

JK: Yeah. He was married to Stella at that point, and Gabrielle was there. That was the first time I had ever met Gabrielle, but she had already had a stroke, and she was in a wheelchair, and kind of in a daze. We managed to track him down by getting in touch with some of the Kerouac's that were in the phone book, which we looked up in a Chinese restaurant, and we got taken to see him by a couple of relatives, Doris and Harvey Kerouac, who were very happy to see me—or seemed so. When I saw Jack—it was the last time—we told him we were going to Mexico. He was drunk, sitting in front of the TV, watching *The Beverly Hillbillies*. He was sitting in a rocking chair, drinking a quart of whisky, with his blue plaid shirt on, and he knew who I was. He said, "Oh yeah! Go to Mexico! You go to Mexico, you can use my name." He knew I was his daughter, but he just had to say that—out of his drunken haze, which I understand. Well, I hadn't really gotten into drinking then yet, but later I practically fell into alcoholism, in Arizona, much later, so I understand the whole mentality.

GN: At that point, when you'd seen him the second time, you'd already had a hell of a life. I mean, you'd really gone through a lot of bad experiences.

JK: The second time? Yeah.

GN: Was there a feeling like maybe Jack was somehow responsible for all this?

JK: No, no, never. That never occurred to me. I always thought that he was just sort of elevated somewhere away from everything—and ...

GN: That he had to be that way?

JK: Yeah, he had to, he was important, he was sort of precious, or he was some kind of a baby. I realized from the very beginning that he needed to be protected from all these things—and I didn't want to bring the harsh reality of my needs to him—and ruin him, 'cause I figured he was some very delicate kind of being that was doing something very important, and that I shouldn't interfere with him. But I definitely would've loved to have known him better, or maybe be his drinking buddy, or whatever—though he might have died even sooner if that was the case.

GN: I doubt it.

JK: Maybe not.

GN: He drank as heavy as you can drink.

JK: I guess so. Well, at one point I did too—but at least I stopped.

GN: So you were in Mexico for a while?

JK: For four months.

GN: And it was fairly soon after you got back that you heard of his death?

JK: Oh, I went to Mexico in October of '67, thinking, expecting to have a baby. Well, I was pregnant, and I got all the way up to 7 months and had a stillbirth. I won't go into all those ramifications of how I felt and everything—that was pretty intense—and then of course the guy I was with wasn't the father of the baby. I came back through San Diego, and then lived with John in San Francisco for a year.

GN: How did you hear about Jack's death?

JK: It was '68 when we lived in San Francisco. Then we moved north of San Francisco, still following my mother, because my mother was trying to make it up to Washington state in time to appear at the hearing—where these people were gonna try and get custody of her daughters. She just didn't make it, though. In fact, Henri Cru, this old friend of Jack's, who I had known earlier, gave my mother a one-way ticket to San Francisco. His motive—that's the funny thing—his motive was to get back at me for not appreciating some stupid Care package that he'd sent me, when I was down and out. Well, I did appreciate it, I just didn't write him back immediately to thank him. And so he thought, "Oh, I'll get back at her by sending her mother a one-way ticket out to San Francisco," because he thought I was still at odds with my mother like I had been when he had known me. He knew me as a rebellious adolescent daughter, who was at odds with her mother. He thought I still was. I've heard a lot of stories about Henri Cru and all these nasty letters, underlined in all different colors of ink, that he's sent all kinds of people. That seems to be his way of participating in the doings of the living—or something—but anyway, I had my share of that with him. And that's how my mother got out to the West Coast. If it wasn't for Henri Cru, she would never have gotten out there probably. But even as it was, she never managed to get up to Washington in time for the hearing, and so she never got custody of her daughters, but she stayed there anyway just in hopes that she might see them someday.

GN: You were married as soon as you got back to the states?

JK: Yeah, just about as soon as I got back I was married in San Francisco.

GN: And you lived there for just about a year then before you heard that Jack died?

JK: Well, he died in '69, and I got married December 3, 1968.

GN: So it's less than a year?

[Break in tape]

GN: This is probably a hard thing for you to answer ... How did you feel hearing of your father's death?

JK: It's not a hard thing ... um ... I mean, it wasn't. What usually happens with me is, whenever I realize something or I learn something, like the death of my baby, for instance, immediately it doesn't strike me. I mean, I'm sure this happens to a lot of people. My immediate reaction is ... "Oh, gee," and you know, I sort of put it into logical terms, and I think of all the pros and cons and realize, "Hmmm ... maybe that's for the best." That's what I did with my baby. And then a day later, the emotional impact'll hit me. And that's what happened with Jack too. I was living in sort of a commune, I mean as close to a commune as I've ever lived. Because John and I, my husband and I, were living with another couple in Little River, California. One day I was out in the garden, and the girl who lived there came running out in a frenzy, and said to me, "Jan, your father just died, I heard it on the radio!" And, I stood there and just looked at her and—just blank, you know, and I looked at her eyes, and she had these sort of tearful eyes, you know, and she was searching me, waiting for me to burst out crying, or something. And I saw this, and so therefore, probably as a kind of defiance, I just stared at her blankly. I said, "Oh." My mind, my mental side, was working, and I said, "That's strange." And inside I was thinking, "*Hmmm*." I did have a feeling, I had a feeling like, *Ah ... gee, I wanted to know him better. Now he's gone and DIED without even asking my permission.* It seemed like, you know, it was kind of a dirty trick, sort of, to go and die without my knowing about it. But since she was standing there gaping at me, waiting for some kind of emotional torrent, it was impossible for me to give her any satisfaction, so I just stood there blankly. And several days later, things started coming around full circle and hitting different little subconscious points and things, and I started having dreams about him, and gradually, it finally hit home as to what happened. It's still really ... well, I'll never really completely realize it ... 'cause it takes forever to realize things like that. Anyway, sometimes I still don't believe that he's dead ... I still believe he's out there somewhere and that I could actually see him. And I have very realistic dreams about him too ... and, lots of them have been incestuous, as, I suppose, is often the case with situations like that. Ah, but anyway .... that's what happened when I found out my father died.

GN: Your mother told me that you fell apart inside when your father died.

JK: She did??? When did she tell you that?

GN: When I was up in Ellensburg.

JK: Well, whaddaya know ... How does she know that? I mean, that's very strange. Maybe she just ... maybe that's just what she thinks happened to me ... you know, I mean, people project things on other people. That's not true. In fact, I think it made me stronger, I mean because I realized that he had died, and I went through the whole mental process of realizing the whole situation that led to his dying, and as much as I could from where I was ... and ah ... You mean she just came out and said that, I mean she didn't say, "I think" or something? She just said: "Jan fell apart when her father died"? I mean ... like a fact or something?

GN: She said you fell apart inside when your father died.

JK: Well that must be what she thinks happened. Funny ... That's not true. Funny how people have ideas of what happens to other people. I think it made me stronger. Well everything that happens to me, I figure, is just one more calcification, you know, added on to life ... because life ... I mean, you start out as this tender little piece of protoplasm, and then after a while, you know, all these little lichens, and calcifications, just build upon you, and that's what old age is ... and you just get tougher and more crustacean-like as time goes on, or ... that implies hardness on the outside, but there's also hardness on the inside, but hardness doesn't necessarily have to mean insensibility. Strength, you know, that's another kind of hardness. Solidarity ....

GN: Well in all this time, did you have any sense of purpose in your life, or any goal in your life?

JK: Sure. I had all kind of different goals. But you know it's hard to just suddenly be born and suddenly be alive and say, "OK, this is my goal!" Because your goal is made up of all kinds of little particles. I mean, I've had millions of goals, and sometimes they all blend together, and sometimes some of them come apart, but basically … well, I know what my goals are now …

GN: Now you seem to have some definite career goals, and a fairly definite sense of yourself as an artist … you write, and may practice drama and sing and dance. At that point, when your father died, did you have some idea of being a writer or artist?

JK: Well, I was a cocoon then—I was in a formative stage, I guess. I knew that I liked gardening at that point. I hadn't gotten interested in linguistics or etymology yet 'cause I was still in the shadow of my first husband, who was kind of an intellectual giant, and taught me a lot of things … and we collaborated on a novel that never got published, called *The Influence*, which we wrote in Mexico with Mexican pens on Mexican paper. It may still be published someday.

GN: So after your father died, was he still a continuing influence on your life?

JK: I'm sure he must have been. I don't see how he could've failed to be. Ah, in fact, when I went traveling in South America, which is after I left my first husband, and got divorced, I very often felt like I was my father in a certain sense. And I felt—I used to have this feeling that I was neuter, that even though I was female on the outside, I always felt more like I was some kind of neuter entity. All the guys on the street naturally noticed that I was female, and did things to announce their discovery that I was female. I very often had this wish that I could just blend in as a kind of masculine bum, so that no one would know who I was and no one would care, so I could just go through life and do things and nobody would bother me. Because when you're a girl, you can't just wander around on railroad tracks or wander around on streets without guys going after you all the time, unless you're very ugly or something, and sometimes I'd even consciously make an effort to make myself unattractive so that guys wouldn't even look at me. I did that a few times, not very often. But it was interesting how it actually does work. I'd bundle myself up with strange rags and stuff and give myself a limp and contort my face, and it's really, truly amazing. Some guys would go by, and they'll look at you and just go right by you. And if you take all those things off and just walk naturally, you'll just be assaulted. It's funny. Anyway, I had a lot of thoughts, a lot of contemplations, on that paradox when I was traveling in South America.

GN: As you got older, you must have realized that your father was a very famous person.

JK: Yeah.

GN: How did you feel knowing that the rest of the world knew your father maybe better than you did? Or just the fact that so many people knew your father, how did that make you feel?

JK: Well, I've had several run-ins with intellectuals, or so-called intellectuals, that have been crazy about my father. In Ellensburg there's one of them. I've always felt contempt for this person, because he seems to be a complete parasite. He doesn't have any kind of self-dignity or anything at all. He's just constantly coming over and saying, "Ooh you're Kerouac's daughter," and asking me all about Kerouac, you know, as if that's all he lives for. I suppose that's justified in a way because my father was really a beacon——

GN: For millions of people.

JK: Yeah, for millions of people, but I don't know, I'm rather hard on people ... I have been in the past. Hard on people I don't understand. I don't really know how to take apart the whole thing of being the daughter of someone famous. I guess it has something to do with the ego of being who you are, not wanting to be part of someone else ... it's really complicated. I don't even know how to begin to talk about it.

GN: Well you're forced to share your father whether you want to or not.

JK: Yeah, and the fact that I never even knew him very well makes me feel sort of noncommittal about it, like, "I dunno!" I mean, I'll just say right out, "Well, I never really knew him very well." The fact that this individual is assuming that I knew all about my father kind of annoys me. Because, no, I didn't know all about my father, and naturally deep down somewhere I kind of resent the fact I didn't know him that well. I don't resent him for not letting me know him that well, but it's just fate, you know, the fact that I just didn't happen to ever manage to know him that well. But these people just assume that since I'm his daughter, I must know all about him. And then there's always that envy of girls who actually have a father who gives them money and is always by their side and does all this stuff. I sort of feel like they had it too easy ... like they're marshmallows or something. They have no problems ... but of course they have the other problems ... but naturally they don't have the one problem that in my life was the ... well, you know, all these are just petty human psychological dilemmas. They're just not worth going into ....

GN: Now you have a very definite sense of yourself as an artist. Is that related to your father at all, or is it you?

JK: It's probably partially my father and partially me. I hope, I mean, I know it's more than just my father. Certainly he is a big part of it because he's part of the fountain from which I spring. But a great deal of it is just my own self.

GN: Do you worry about that, that it may be hard to come out from under his shadow, or to disassociate yourself, or to have people read your stuff on your own terms? Do you feel like maybe it will always be very difficult for people just to relate to you directly and not judge your work or relate it in any way to Jack?

JK: I know I have my own style of writing, which is very different from Jack's. It's similar to his in some ways, but I'm not as subjective as he is. I'm more objective. I think it has to do with the fact that he was Pisces and I'm an Aquarius. He was very emotional and very watery, and everything he saw was directly related, I mean directly attached to his soul. Whereas with me, I tend to think, which is not necessarily a good thing always—sometimes quite the contrary—but I tend to always think things out. Maybe I think them out so much sometimes that they become muddy with thought … No, I'm not that worried about shining out from under his shadow. I mean, his shadow is qualified … if I can manage to shine out from underneath it, then that's OK, that's good—and if I can't, well, tough. If people are reading my stuff and thinking, "Well, this is Jack Kerouac's daughter, let's see if she's as good as he is" … I don't even think it's necessary to make a comparison like that because I wasn't trying to emulate his type of writing anyway. In fact, three years ago, when I started writing this book, I just had an idea … I just thought, "Gee, I've actually done enough things in my life that it actually warrants writing about it." And so I had this big brainstorm one night drinking tea, about this book that I could write. I figured it all out, and I started writing, and after a while I found that I liked writing. It turned out pretty well. And I'm not trying to write the way he does, although sometimes I tend to sort of slip into certain things that are similar to the way he writes, but I think it's kind of hereditary or something, it just happens … and I'm more conservative, I think … I'm more conventional in the way I write … I don't have astronomical run-on sentences like he did. I'm tempted to do it sometimes, and maybe I will do a few of them just for the fun of it, 'cause he's not the only one who's ever done it. But I am, it's true, a little bit hesitant to do things like that, just for the sheer fact that people might think that, "Ah she's just trying to copy her father." I'm trying to rise above that fear. It's not that big a fear, though, it's just a little thing that holds me back. I haven't read that much of his stuff, so I don't feel like I'm in danger of being too terribly influenced by his writing.

GN: I'm curious about that one editor that looked at your work and felt that your writing, or at least this one autobiographical novel you're writing, seems to be kind of a quest to find your father.

JK: Who was that?

GN: That was Christopher Buckley at *Esquire*.

JK: Oh.

GN: Do you agree with that—do you think he was right? ... He thought your writing was a search for your father.

JK: You know, he might be kinda right, now that I think of it. I mean, all these travels that I've been on, there might be some truth in that ... I never really thought about it before, but it might just be something organic, you know, something out of my control that I'm doing that I haven't even intellectualized. 'Cause I know that traveling around and feeling this desire to be male or at least neuter, so that people don't notice me as much, or alternately off and on enjoying being female and yet wishing that I was male, definitely has something to do with my father and a lack of his presence. But I don't dwell on it all the time. I figure if it's there, it's there. And if I spent all my time thinking about it, it would be a disaster.

GN: I'm also curious how you feel about your father's sudden rise to notoriety after having been forgotten largely for many years.

JK: Huh?

GN: Now, of course, he's the subject of several biographies, and you were at the awards dinner of the National Society of Arts and Letters because of a biography about him ....

JK: Mm-hmmm....

GN: How do you feel about that, that all of a sudden everybody seems to want to get in on the act?

JK: That's the way everything always happens. Naturally I couldn't just break out with some off-the-wall autobiography of something I did just because I'm his daughter ... at first I thought maybe I could do that, but I'm realizing it's not possible, because I'm a little too far removed from the focus of interest, and what happens is, it's like wine, it's aged long enough now. Things go in generations, go in fits and starts, and suddenly a little element of society, or a huge element, comes around to a certain state of mind and gradually gets to a point where they're enriched by something that happened a long time ago—like Shakespeare.

All kinds of different authors are constantly coming back in cycles. And I'm sure anyone would be hard put to analyze why that happens in complete detail. It's just like breathing. The whole world, the literary world, is just breathing. And there are in-breaths and out-breaths, I mean inhalations and exhalations, and it just happens. It's great. I'm glad that they're suddenly remembering him again.

GN: Well if your father very soon becomes famous, as seems to be likely because all his books have come back into print within the last two years and——

JK: Re-famous.

GN: Re-famous, yeah, and famous in a more lasting way because he was famous then just as kind of a cult figure, a leader of beatniks. But now that they're going to start filming a lot of his books, and people are going to be writing critically about his books, and he may really be given a very high place, a lasting place in American literature, how's that going to affect you? I mean, will it affect you at all?

JK: Well, it probably will affect me … just by the very fact that I have his name. In various ways it'll affect me because I know he's my father and I realize that he's becoming famous again, which'll do something to my subconscious—but that's not as important. Well, in a way that's more important—to me. But on a large scale, it might affect me because I might get some notoriety because of my name, and my book might sell. Well, it will sell eventually, hopefully sooner than later, and even though it's not mainly about him, he comes in when he comes in, just in the same proportion as he came in, as he influenced my life, in reality, because the whole book is about my life—as it's happened so far. Sure, it'll affect me somehow—hopefully for the better. Hopefully it'll affect somebody somehow.

GN: Do you see art as your permanent profession now?

JK: Oh yeah! Definitely. Art. Oh yeah, yeah. I know I'm majoring in Spanish, that's for sure. I'll probably learn French by and by, somewhere along the line. I'll go to Paris or something, but I'd like to learn French-

Canadian also, because that's what he spoke. I'm always interested in little dialects and little offshoots of languages—but somehow or other I wound up in the Spanish stream by going down to South America and always being around Puerto Ricans in New York, and then living in New Mexico and Mexico. Spanish is very important somehow. It really figures into my life, and I might even wind up writing in Spanish, teaching in Spanish, or something. I know something's gonna happen in that line. But then, besides that, I paint, and I definitely write—I sing and I dance. I guess the humanities is definitely gonna be my area—as it is with a lot of people.

GN: Do you regret any part of your past?

JK: No. Well maybe I just say that this moment. Let me think, let me dig a little deeper. I suppose the first impression would be the most accurate. When I just said "No," I mean there's no sense in regretting anything.

GN: Do you feel it's all gonna be useful to you somehow as a writer?

JK: Sure. I mean, why regret any part of your past, you know? Your past is the foundation on which your life is built—and if you regret your past, it's just senseless. I suppose I could say, if I was gonna be very sentimental, I regret not having known Jack better—my father, I should say. Yeah, I suppose I could say I regret that, but then in the same breath I realize that there was a reason for everything that happened. There was a reason for him dying when he did—and a reason for everything!

GN: Seeing as though you may soon become a famous artist in your own right, how do you think you'll react to that? You may soon be in the position that Jack was.

JK: Well, it would be nice after all these years of being on welfare—and washing dishes. I wouldn't mind a little money, and a change of pace. I'm sure I could find something to do with it. There are so many things that I want to do. If I had more resources, I could do more things. I could also help my mother out, who's been in destitute poverty for years and years and years and years. She's been poorer than I have all this time. I've never had the experience like most young people, you know, always going to their parents to borrow money and stuff. I haven't the slightest idea how that is, because my mother has always been poorer than I am—and so when I come home, it's like coming home to—I don't even know how to describe it. Well, I did describe it in my book, so I won't even repeat it here. I'm always lending her money and stuff. She's really had a hard time, but she's also been enriched by the whole fiasco, or whatever you want to call it.

GN: Do you feel writing is going to be the way for you, or are you going to try other arts?

JK: Oh, I'll try other things, but I like writing. I'm definitely going to finish this book and perhaps write maybe a few others too, because I guess it's usually the case. Now that I've started writing, all these other ideas are coming to me—and I'll probably follow them through, but there's so many other things—so many other mediums that I'd like to pursue, or that I like to work in, like painting, pottery, and the things that I've dabbled in, that I'd like to go farther with. Acting, certainly—that's one of the biggest ones—and singing.

GN: The practice of art made your father's life very difficult. Are you afraid that it might make your life difficult?

JK: It made his life difficult?

GN: It made it difficult to stay married.

JK: Ugghh!

GN: Or to cement personal relationships.

JK: Well, difficult in that sense I don't think is difficult. I mean, married—that's mundanity! That's the way I see it. I've been married twice, and I'm in the process of getting a divorce right now. I think art is much more important than anything like that. Well, it depends on the situation, you know? Who knows? I might fall in love and get married again—

because I have very weak will power and I do things on the spur of the moment. But my general view of marriage and things like that ... no, I shouldn't even say anything about that. Then again, my first marriage, especially, was very nice. I gained a lot from that. I learned a lot from my first marriage, but I was much younger than my first husband. I was fifteen, he was twenty-two, and naturally we grew older in that ratio. And then my second husband was as young in relation to me as I had been to my first husband—so maybe that was some kind of compensation or something. All I can do is speak for myself. I think that freedom, individuality, and doing whatever you feel like—and writing, painting, and traveling, especially—is more important than staying in one little town, and keeping house and being cemented to one person just because they think you ought to. I think freedom is very important.

GN: You said that in some sense your writing was a quest to find your father. Do you feel now that you've gotten somewhat closer to him?

JK: Well, yeah. Of course it's very ethereal, it's very hard to pinpoint. But as my life progresses, naturally I'll probably become closer and closer to him, because everything will become more and more manifest—Jack included. I mean, I'll be closer to everything, except birth. Sure, I'll learn more and more about him. I am learning more and more about him—especially since I've run into you, and since I've started writing this book and meeting all these people involved with him. Before I started writing the book, I hadn't met so many people that knew him or knew of him. Now I'm learning of him vicariously, I'm learning all these things about him I always suspected anyway—because I've had a kind of natural intuition about what he was like and how he felt about things anyway. And now they're all just being confirmed.

GN: Do you have any bitterness in the sense that he's being recognized now and he wasn't in his lifetime?

JK: Well, yeah, I've been thinking about that lately—but I have a feeling that wherever he is, now that he's not alive any more—I really believe that he knows what's happening. I mean, I believe that he realizes that he's being recognized in his absence, just like Shakespeare and all kinds of people have been. I think the soul must know about that when that happens—but then I have some pretty weird ideas about reincarnation and stuff.

GN: Of course he always said that.

JK: Really?

GN: He always said that he was like Shakespeare and that he was gonna be recognized much more after his death.

JK: He probably knew it already then.

GN: Yeah, he knew it.

JK: Yeah, so I can perfectly imagine the same thing happening to me— or anybody. And who knows? I was so used to living in poverty that it really didn't matter. I'm perfectly prepared to live that way the rest of my life, if it happens, because I know how to live that way. Therefore, if I come across some fortune, or if I come upon good times or something like that, I'll just be pleasantly surprised, but if I don't, then I won't be terribly disappointed. Because you can be just as happity in povery— you know? I mean, I always was. We had great times drinking Lipton's tea and watching the cockroaches and eating Chef Boyardee spaghetti and whatever. Those are some of the greatest times in my life—living in the Lower East Side, and being poor—because then all your senses are more highly tuned, or they were in my case.

GN: Would you have exchanged your father for anybody else?

JK: No! I had several father substitutes that sort of filled in in his absence. His absence was just all-encompassing because that's all there was ... except for those two incidents. But my mother had certain beaus—maybe I should call them—that were delightful, especially one, Harry Peace. I don't even know what to say about him. He was very entertaining. He'd been all around the world, and he had all kinds of stories to tell, and he was an alcoholic, just like most everyone we knew on the Lower East Side—an alcoholic or a junkie. They were very intense people, who had a lot of feelings. Perhaps they were trying to hide a lot of their feelings by doing what they did.

GN: Do you think your father was hiding his feelings?

JK: He must have been hiding them, definitely. And one of those feelings, one of those secrets, was me! I know that. I could just tell by looking at him, and by everything I've heard from all the friends of his that talked about him and what they knew of him. It was just one of those unfortunate things, you know? You tell somebody a lie, like your mother, for instance. Well, that's pretty important. He told his mother a kind of a lie to protect her feelings. That's perfectly understandable, and in later life he had to keep up the lie to protect her further, and it's just one of those things, you know? He couldn't take it back because he was tied to her in certain ways—that's just the way it happened. But it was probably best the way it happened, 'cause everything always is best the way it happens, 'cause that's the way it's supposed to happen. If he had hung around and been a father to me, he wouldn't have written all his books. He wouldn't have gotten all that inspiration. He might have gotten different inspiration, but he didn't. No, I'm perfectly happy to be the missing element that enabled him to be who he was. That in itself is a kind of a stigma. Of course I'm looking at it from the point of view of the future looking into the past, and seeing how it happened. But if I had been his daughter, and if he had stuck around and been my father, maybe he wouldn't have written all the things that he wrote, and therefore I wouldn't even be able to think in those terms because he wouldn't have written them so I wouldn't even have known about that. It's very hard to talk about if's. I always get very confused. I mean, I go into long tirades about fate and stuff whenever I talk about if's—I just can't avoid it. I wonder what else I should say.

GN: I think you've said quite a lot.

JK: Yeah—I've said too much probably! ... Should I say something about Chicago? Let's see, what can I say about Chicago? Well, as a native New Yorker, I think Chicago sucks! When I first came to Chicago in the wintertime last winter, well maybe it has something to do with the fact that I arrived at the Greyhound bus station, but I perceived Chicago as being rather obnoxious! But then again, any city of any magnitude should be obnoxious. I mean, if it's not obnoxious, it's not a city!

GN: Can I quote you on that?

JK: Sure. How can a city exist without being obnoxious? It wouldn't be a city. So OK, I was walking around trying to buy some cigarettes in the drugstore and struggling around between a whole crowd of black baseball fanatics—or was it football or something? And practically being knocked into the street and assaulted by weirdos, and feeling very alien because I had just come from New York and I wasn't used to Chicago, and so I was noticing the el and all that stuff, which took me back to childhood when New York had an el—and I lived next to it—and it seemed sort of nightmarish somehow. And I sort of thought, *Uugghhhh!* You know? *It's weird here.* Well, *naturally!*

[Tape ends.]

ABOUT THE AUTHORS

Lynbrook, Long Island native Lynn Kushel Archer has been a long-time friend and supporter of many Beat writers, including Paul Krassner, Kirby Doyle, Jack Micheline, and Martin Matz. She currently raises bees and surfs the web in Forest Knolls, California.

John Allen Cassady, named after Jack Kerouac and Allen Ginsberg, was the son of Beat heroes Neal and Carolyn Cassady. He has lectured on the Beats all over the country in the Beat Museum's traveling Beatmobile, and he is the author of a memoir of his father called *Visions of Neal: A Boy's Life With His Father.*

Phil Cousineau has written and produced numerous films and books, including the award-winning documentary *The Hero's Journey: Joseph Campbell—A Biographical Portrait* and the best-selling *The Art of Pilgrimage: The Seeker's Guide to Making Travel Sacred.*

Mary Emmerick is a Chicago journalist and authored many of the original *Ann Landers* columns.

Born in Israel, Adiel Gorel is the President and CEO of International Capital Group, a prominent real estate investment firm located in San Rafael, California, and is a nationally-renowned lecturer on gaining wealth through real estate. A Stanford engineering graduate, he is also the author of two books, *Remote-Controlled Real Estate Riches—The Busy Person's Guide to Real Estate Investing* and *Discovering Real Estate in America.* Much like Jan Kerouac, he has traveled extensively throughout Mexico, South America and other parts of the world, and speaks several languages.

A noted voice actor in Los Angeles and dubbed "the Hollywood historian" by the *Los Angeles Times*, six-foot-four gentle giant and monster aficionado Lee Harris was Jan Kerouac's last heartthrob.

Jacques Kirouac is the founding president of L'Association des Familles Kirouac. A retired professor and director of Graduate Studies at Laval University, he lives in Quebec City. He too is a world traveler.

A former acquisitions editor of Conari Press, Brenda Knight assembled and edited the landmark anthology *Women of the Beat Generation*. She lives and writes in San Francisco, across the street from where Jack Kerouac wrote his greatest novel, *Visions of Cody*.

Former Chicagoan Carl Macki was the publisher of the legendary *X* magazine. For the past 25 years, he has been a dadaist poet in the Bay Area of California. He writes regularly for *Punk Globe* magazine, and promotes poetry and music events throughout the Bay Area.

Dan McKenzie's father was a Scot and his mother a Yoeme and Chiricahua Apache (called Yaqui in Mexico) Indian. A potter and poet, he lives in Cotati, California. His first book of poetry, *Ghost Chants* from Enchanted Horse Press, was a cult classic. He also served in the United States Marines in Vietnam in 1968, and is active in the pursuit of recognition and just treatment for America's veterans.

Knoxville singer/songwriter R.B. Morris has been praised by everyone from Bobby Neuwirth to *Playboy Magazine*, and has been compared to everyone from Townes Van Zandt to John Prine and Tom Waits.

Gerald Nicosia is the author of *Memory Babe: A Critical Biography of Jack Kerouac*, called a "great book" by Allen Ginsberg and recently hailed by both the *Chicago Sun-Times* and the *London Times* as still the best biography of Jack Kerouac. He remained friends with Jan Kerouac from their first meeting in June, 1978, until her death 18 years later.

Lowell, Massachusetts native Brad Parker founded the Lowell Corporation for the Humanities, which produced many notable cultural events around Lowell's historical and literary figures. The author of several scholarly monographs, including *Kerouac: An Introduction*, he currently teaches in Japan.

John Paul Pirolli, a.k.a. The Buddah, is—by his own admission—a "Gnostic priest, poet, playwright, musician, magician, artist, fartist, joker, toker, tobacco smoker, enigma wrapped in a question, tidewater shit shoveler, and fat buddha with a fiendish grin and Rasputin eyes." He is also President of the Board of The Stone Soup Poetry Society in Boston; founder of the Barnum and Buddah Poetry Circus; and a member of The Fire of Prometheus Poetry Troupe as well as the Unbearables poetry group in New York City. From 1997-2000, he produced and hosted *The Rebel Café* radio show on Radio Free Cambridge in Cambridge, Massachusetts. His first book of poetry, *Madman on the Merrimac*, was published by Alpha Beat Press in 1994.

Aram Saroyan, son of William Saroyan, is a novelist, poet, essayist, and playwright. His writing has earned many awards, and he currently teaches in the Masters of Professional Writing Program at USC. He is among those few select individuals who have lived to see their father honored on a U.S. postage stamp.

Dr. John Zielinski runs his own medical clinic on the South Side of Chicago. On his off nights, he has been glimpsed playing blues and sometimes boogie-woogie piano at the Old Town Ale House.

COLOPHON

Jan Kerouac: A Life in Memory was designed and typeset by Luz Decker in San Francisco. It was printed and bound in December, 2008, by James Barrios of DeHart's Media Services in Santa Clara, California.

26 copies, lettered A-Z, were signed by Gerald Nicosia and Phil Cousineau, with artwork by Jan Kerouac tipped in.